Parenting in My Pocket

Parenting Q&A

vol. 2

To Louise,

Thanks for all
the support!

Best Wishes,

Transcription by: Julie Stevenson
Book Design by: Maria C. A. Fowler
Photo credits: Toddler image by Krakenimages
on Unsplash.com

Ebook ISBN: 978-1-8382593-3-4
Paperback ISBN: 978-1-8382593-2-7

www.helpme2parent.ie

Parenting
in My Pocket

Parenting
Q & A
vol. 2

by Allen O'Donoghue

**Help Me
To Parent**

To Con, Mary, Colin & Helen,
thank you for all the support over the years!

Table of Contents

About the Q & A Format

Over the years of working with families, I would regularly get questions sent to me via every channel there is. I have always committed to answering every question I get, as I believe that if someone takes the time to email me, it's obviously a big enough issue for them and they deserve a reply. I then started to think about how beneficial these questions and answers might be to others, and so the seeds of the Live Q & A were first sown. In 2018, I decided to take the plunge and start dealing with questions live, and I thoroughly enjoyed the process. From the feedback that's come our way, many parents have found some reassurance knowing that others have experienced similar issues with bringing up their children.

The Parenting In My Pocket weekly video is now carrying on the mantle and is building week-on-week. Thank you to every parent who has sent in questions over the years, this book wouldn't be here without you.

ACTIVITIES

Q. Kids birthday parties! Now my oldest has started Primary 1, she has been bringing home party invitations it seems daily! I've had to buy four separate kids' birthday presents for just this weekend alone. My own daughter's birthday party is only a couple weeks away, and selfishly, that is my highest priority on the present-buying budget. Then there are some parties that require fancy dress where I have to buy a specific outfit and the done thing seems to be to invite the whole class to the party.

For my daughter's birthday I told her she could pick nine friends from school and to be honest she struggled to think of nine kids she played with, she's only been at school for four weeks. I have already had comments from some parents wondering why their child wasn't invited when so-and-so's was, and tried to explain that I wanted my daughter to have the birthday party she wanted with people she knew.

So my questions are: Is it really necessary to invite every child in the class to the party? Do you think it's unfair for the other children who she doesn't know or play with? And also how much is enough to spend on a present when you're buying so many?

A. Let's deal with the first question asked. No, it's not necessary to invite every child from your daughter's class to the party. Parents listen up, it's not necessary and we shouldn't make other parents feel guilty for not doing so. There is no need to put ourselves under so much pressure, especially financially, to invite everyone to the party and it's also not necessary to put that pressure on a child, especially in this circumstance where they haven't been in the school that long.

A lot of schools are pulling away from allowing children to bring invites into class for their parties as some children don't get invited, and this can make them feel left out and put pressure on the birthday child to answer questions from non-invited children that they may not be able to answer. Schools are now getting parents to get in touch with other parents regarding invites.

If you feel strongly about the class invitation process you could get in touch with the school and see what the policy is. I'm sure your child's teacher is well aware of when invites get distributed.

Don't worry about other parents' attitude towards your decision; this is your child and you are doing what is best for you and your family. Other parents may do things differently and that's up to them, just concentrate on your own family.

In regard to your next question, it's perfectly acceptable not to invite the children your child doesn't play with. If your child is playing with a number of children regularly and their names come up in conversation a bit, these are the children you want to get to know first. Friendships change from week to week sometimes, and you may have a different set of friends at the party the following year!

It's not your responsibility to make sure that other people's children have friends. You, of course, teach your child to be nice to others, and if they saw a child on their own in the playground, you would encourage them to play together, but that's teaching a lesson in kindness.

Finally, in regard to the amount spent on presents, this is something you could bring up at a school meeting as a discussion topic. There would be many parents who would find the financial burden of party gifts overwhelming but don't want their child to be the odd one out in terms of money spent. You would be amazed to see and hear the collective sigh of relief if a parent put forward a more financially acceptable solution to the problem.

If approaching the school isn't possible, and as you will have a contact list for parents of children, you could put out a simple text suggesting a cap on spend for each gift or to possibly pool the money together and buy one big gift or give the child the money?

If your child is invited to nearly all of their classmates' parties in one year, this can add up to a huge amount of money that isn't budgeted for in most households. Suggesting a budget or even that no presents are given is a way forward and will help out a lot of parents who may be feeling the pressure.

We need to be realistic about children's parties. Most children just want to have fun with their friends and are not focusing on the gifts or money they will receive, and it is the parent's responsibility to see this and give an appropriate amount towards each gift.

Q. My ten-year-old son is addicted to Lego®. While I don't mind this too much as he gets so much joy from it, he's starting to not want to go out and play with his friends and just wants to do his Lego® all the time. Even homework is becoming an issue as all he thinks about is his Lego®. How can I help him see that he needs balance?

A. It's lovely to see that your son has a passion for Lego®; he's using his imagination and skills to build and isn't stuck in front of the TV or on a device. These are all the positives associated with your son's hobby.

Of course, you're right, there needs to be a balance for your son. His hobby is not bad, but like doing too much of any one one thing, can lead to problems, and as you have noticed, he is shutting himself away from the world a bit.

You can sit down with your son and discuss how you have noticed his behaviour change and that although you are so happy that he enjoys his Lego®, he also needs to do his homework and get fresh air and play with his friends. You can let him know that there will always be time put aside for him to play Lego®, but he needs to do other things too. He needs to know that his pastime is really important, and you know how much he loves it. You're not threatening to take this away from him, but there needs to be a balance, and you are concerned he's not getting that at the moment.

If you are worried about his social interaction with other children, see if there is a local Lego® club. A number of schools now have after-school Lego® clubs as it is so popular. He will meet like-minded children and could possibly strike up some great friendships.

You will need to set up some boundaries around the Lego®. Let him know what chores or work needs to be done before he can play with his Lego® and then let him know how long he can play for. Hopefully he will see where you are coming from and that you are not trying to punish him, but are trying to give him a more balanced life.

Summertime Activities

When summertime is approaching, we are looking forward to a bit of time off, maybe going away on holidays, sunshine, and time to relax, but our children are also around more and the days can become very long, so we need to do a little bit of forward planning and come up with a list of things that we can do with our children to help keep them entertained and you sane.

Toddlers/Younger Kids

Toddlers are a funny age group, they have boundless energy and some days there just aren't enough activities to exhaust them! They are full of fun, entertainment, and curiosity.

While you may all be looking forward to a break and change from the normal routine—the same mundane day-to-day tasks like dinners and washing—bedtimes will still continue. It's important to structure in some time to get these bits out of the way, let the children know that you are doing them, and have something fun planned for later in the day or early in the day, whichever suits your family best.

Here are a few ideas that may help you.

Routine is important: Try and keep the routine as close to normal as possible, especially for toddler and younger children, as it's important they get their naps and a good solid night's sleep in order to be able to function properly the next day and not be tired and upset. It's also important that mealtimes are kept around the same time as this is what their little bodies are used to. Parents of younger children are usually up earlier regardless of the time of year it is, and children usually go to bed earlier, too, so try and keep that normal routine going. It will of course be a little bit more relaxed as you may not be rushing children out to playschool.

Of course, it's normal to want to take the foot off the pedal a bit and change things up when you are on holidays or school is out, but changing the routine for younger children is confusing for them and by the time you get to late August/early September and school again, there will be extra work and very tired children as you may need to start their routine all over again.

Summertime doesn't have to cost a fortune. There are, of course, loads of summer camps that are put on for all age groups and can vary in price, and these are really beneficial to parents who are working and need to have their children looked after outside of the house. Schools and crèches may also run summer camps, especially in the early weeks of the summer. It's a source of income for the school, and your children will be comfortable going as they know where it is and more than likely some of their friends will be there too. If you can find camps that you can afford and your children will enjoy, they can be a brilliant way to break up the long weeks of the summer and take the pressure off you to provide the entertainment or look for alternative childcare.

Paddling Pools/Water

Nothing better in the summer on hot sticky days than being able to splash about in a paddling pool eating ice pops. Water guns are also a great way to have some fun with your children or for them to have fun together. All children love getting their parents wet and they will remember the fun forever.

You can set little rules around not getting parents wet if they are in normal clothes but if they are in play-time clothes, then it's all out water fight. Don't forget to be safe around water, even small amounts in a paddling pool. Never leave small children unattended or in the care of older children.

Learning to Cycle

If you are a parent at home, have the time, and your child is at the age to get on a bike, then help them learn to cycle. Most households have a bike in the shed, or if not, there will definitely be one in a relative's house. Neighbours on the street will be more than happy to lend a bike. Don't forget the helmet!

Painting Days/Street Chalk

Big sheets of paper, cheap roll of wallpaper, and large sticks of chalk are great ways of letting your child paint outside and have fun. Paths in front of your house or even the drive way are a great place to use the chalk and it washes away as soon as the next rain shower comes along. Make life-sized drawings of each other and colour them in.

Rainy Days

Movie days are lovely—cuddles on the sofa and their favourite treats. Baking simple buns or Rice Krispies® buns with their choice of toppings is lots of fun and they will be learning new skills too.

Building forts and dens with all the cushions and blankets in the house is also a great way to have fun and they can help with the tidy up.

More Ideas

Other ways to spend the time over the holidays could include trips to visit family, going to the local play park, take a trip on the train or bus, or, even if you have a swimming pool nearby, learning how to swim.

Having a list of activities, big or small, can help to give you ideas on how to spend the day when the children are at home. Remember to not try and do everything in one day, or feel the need to entertain your child all day. They, too, will need rest times and may just want to watch a few cartoons. Look at your day and see when an activity may come in handy and plan it out, get them involved, take your time, and enjoy the experience.

If you are a working parent and may only have a couple of weeks off during the summer then this list might be beneficial to whoever is caring for your child unless they are going to a creche as they usually have loads of fun summer activities planned.

Older Kids/Preteens

For this age group, summer camps or youth clubs are a great way to keep them entertained. They don't have to be overly expensive, lots of them will be run by your local sports club or even their school. Most places will start to advertise their camps a couple of months before the schools finish up, so keep an eye out and maybe you could spread the cost of them so it's not one big chunk of money all at one go.

Your child may protest about some of the camps they may need to go to, but it will be something new for them and they may surprise themselves.

Games

Let them get creative, challenge them to make entertainment for themselves. Get them to make football goals, create games with chalk sticks and send them out into the fresh air. Buy a cheap tent for them and let them use it as a den, even stay out all night in the back garden.

Get them to clean their rooms and then anything they don't want to keep, they could set up a little stall in the front garden and sell their old stuff, they might even make enough for a week's worth of ice-cream!

Relatives

Send them off to their grandparents or another relative who might need some help around the house or garden. When children are a bit older there is less minding of them to do, so they are well able to get to work and it's a great opportunity for them to spend time with other family and learn more about them.

Cooking

Get creative in the kitchen! Children are fantastic cooks, and as long as you are there to oversee the use of cookers and kettles, they will be able to bake or even make the dinner. They will learn so many new skills and be proud of themselves for making something that tastes really good. Don't be worrying about mess and the cleaning up, it's part of the process and many hands make light work.

Make & Do

Could you find some small woodwork projects for them to do like a bird house or letterbox, that they could nail together, paint and hang? It wouldn't take too much time or need many materials, and it's something they could do themselves with a little guidance from a parent.

Are there jobs around the garden or home that they could earn a bit of pocket money out of like painting fences, cutting the grass or helping clear out an attic?

A little bit of preparation on your side will make finding things for this age group to do a lot easier as the summer approaches. They will know what's coming up and also when there will be days off as it's just important that they get to recharge their batteries after the school year. Rainy days are great for vegging under the duvet and watching movies!

Teenagers

Camps

Summer camps are a great option for teenagers, especially younger teens who need to be out and supervised for part of the day. Local youth groups or centres will run a number of activities during the summer months with plenty of different options. There will definitely be at least one camp that your child would be interested in and then there may be others that they should give a go just to try something different. Usually these camps organise day trips away too.

Camps Away From Home

If you have the funds, Irish college or a camp that is based away from home for a couple of weeks or more is a really good option. They will learn so much about themselves, living with others, and meeting new people as they will be away from home.

Rest in Morning/Activity in the Afternoon

If your teenagers don't usually surface until lunchtime and you are ok with it, then that's fine, maybe there will be something for them to get involved in during the afternoons. Don't forget teenagers needs their rest to recharge their brains and their bodies after the school year, so a little bit of relaxing the rules is necessary.

Voluntary Work/Help Family

There could be voluntary work that your child could get involved in. Some primary schools are more than happy to have past pupils back in the school to help out, especially in June when they are finishing up for the year and the school needs to be tidied up before closing.

Most towns will have a Volunteers Centre that are always looking for people to help out even if it is just during the summer, and you could agree to give them a wage every week for doing the work.

Are there jobs that grandparents need help with, or other family members that might be able to bring them to work to help out?

Summer Job

If they are old enough, then a summer job is a really good option for a teenager. It will give them independence, work experience, their own money, and a real sense of having achieved something. If they do a little bit of work handing in CVs to places, they might like to work a couple of months before the summer then they could easily get a job. If they are involved in a sports club that is running camps, they may need coaches or help to run the camps.

ANXIETY

Q. My five-year-old used to be very confident, and still can be at times, but recently she seems to have developed severe performance anxiety. She can be a bit of a perfectionist, and I think it's a fear of doing something wrong in front of people and everyone seeing her make a mistake.

She takes part in some classes and clubs: gymnastics, swimming, and Girls' Brigade, and enjoys going to them and participating. However, she flat out refuses to do any competitions, shows, or performances. I didn't mind so much with the clubs as long as she was going weekly and taking part in the classes, but now she has told me that she isn't going to take part in the school nativity. I didn't expect her to volunteer for a speaking part, but she is refusing to go on stage at all, even to sing in a big group with the rest of her class. She says that it will be too scary to do it with everyone looking at them. I've tried to talk her into it, re-minding her that she won't be alone, she'll have her whole class beside her, and her best friend will be there with her, but she just gets really upset and then says she doesn't want to talk about it anymore.

I don't really know what to do because, on one hand, I don't want to force her to do something if it upsets her this much, especially if forcing her to do it will just make her worse. But on the other hand, I know that the only way to get over the fear is to do it, and singing in a large group seems like a reasonable compromise to me. I feel like once she does it she'll realise it's not as scary as she has built it up to be in her mind.

A. Here we have a child who has become a lot more aware of herself, and with that, has become more conscious of the spotlight being on her. This is something that is quite normal and natural for a child to experience. What I mean by this is that a child is a baby, then toddler, and the whole world revolves around them. They know few others in their world apart from family and a few playmates. Then they go to playschool, or start school, and they are seeing a lot more people, people they don't know but they have to be around every day. For some children this is great, more people to play with and get to know, but for some children it is difficult, and they would prefer to stay in the background and don't want to step forward and be noticed.

For this parent, they need to get the balance right for their child. Years ago, a child would have been told where they are going, what they are doing, and they have to do it whether or not they like it. Nowadays, we are more aware of what our children are feeling and want to make situations as comfortable as possible for them and not let them feel overwhelmed.

Firstly, all types of personalities and people make up this world. Some people are introverted, some are extroverted, and it's learning to do what's best for each individual in order to get the best out of them and for them to feel good about themselves. In school, teachers try to encourage all children to experience something different or new, and most will. Some children who may have been reluctant to participate, build up the courage to find that they really enjoy the new experiences, and this, in turn, can help their confidence and perhaps make them quicker to volunteer to do something new in the future.

We have to expose our children to all sorts of environments and experiences, in a safe and secure way, to help them develop, become more resilient, and enjoy the great things this life has to offer.

Something has made your child feel unsure, self-conscious, and reluctant to share her talents. She may be feeling vulnerable, and unfortunately the world we live in still sees vulnerability as a weakness and our feelings are not talked about or validated, which for an adult can be difficult, but for a child who is unable to label feelings and verbalise them in the same way, this can be extremely upsetting. Your child may feel that it is safer to do nothing as she isn't aware that what she is feeling, like anxiety or nervousness, is normal, and that talking about it could make her feel better.

I would suggest trying to talk to her about how she is feeling, using language that she can understand. Perhaps a picture book showing expressions of different feelings might help her. Let her know that what she is feeling is ok and that you are there to help her overcome them. Maybe read through the play with her, taking on the other roles, so that she becomes used to saying the lines and it's just normal for her to do it.

If the school is getting in touch after you've helped her, and you feel she is ready to do the play, but they are saying she is still very nervous, upset, and not wanting to do it, you may need to look at other tools to help her. There is a practice called Logosynthesis® that can help to channel her nervous energy into a feeling that can help her to perform on stage and overcome the nerves.

Try not to let this build up into something bigger than it may actually be, as your daughter may pick up on your worry and concern for her, and this could make the situation worse. Sit down and chat to her about times when you felt nervous or anxious about something you had to do and the tools you used to get over it. Let her know how it's ok to be nervous, but that challenging ourselves and overcoming hurdles can make us so much stronger and make the next challenge easier. Children learn so much from their parents and put a lot of faith and trust in what you say to them, so maybe hearing your stories may help her to overcome some of her fears. We have more of an impact on our children's lives than we realise.

You may also need to look at your own family set up and how important perfection is to all of you. Is this something that is expected in the family and perhaps your daughter is feeling this and doesn't want to disappoint? It may not be the case, but it's good to check in and see; sometimes we don't realise how we are acting until we need to look at ourselves and what we are doing. We need our children to know that mistakes happen, it's normal and ok because we learn from them, and that is how we prepare for life. Don't forget your daughter is only 5 and has lots to learn. This is a small section of her life that you need to help her overcome and that's what we are there to do as parents.

Q. I am due my first child in five weeks and I'm really excited and also really nervous about the new arrival. One of the biggest things that is getting to me is my husband. He keeps making remarks that "this baby won't change [his] lifestyle," and how he's still going to keep up his weekly golf, and going out with the lads a couple of times a week. I have no idea what to expect and I'm worried that I'll be left alone to do everything to do with the baby, with very little support. We don't have family living close by, and I find myself feeling quite anxious and lonely at the thoughts of having to do this all by myself. Have you any tips on how to get him to realise how important he is in doing this with me?

A. This is really tough for you. This is one of the biggest things you will do as a couple, and there are so many unknowns about having a baby that makes it an unsettling but exciting time. You have probably heard all sorts of horror stories from friends and family about having a baby, and this can make you feel even more anxious.

So you have 5 weeks to go till baby arrives. You are probably close to finishing work, feeling tired and uncomfortable as baby is a good size now, and you have this worry at the back of your mind. There are parents who believe that having a baby won't change their life, could be mum or dad who feels this way, but as soon as baby arrives, priorities change. That's not to say that your life is over and you can't enjoy the same things as before, it's just going to be different and will need a bit more organising. All of a sudden little baby arrives and they consume every waking minute, in a good way. You can't take your eyes off them and are completely in love. Your partner may be feeling anxious, too, has seen his friends who have children disappear, and doesn't want this to happen to him. He may be worried about being a dad and how he will deal with it, and maybe both of you just haven't had these conversations around how you are feeling before the baby arrives.

None of us know how we are going to react to becoming a parent, how we will deal with it. Don't get into an argument with your partner at the moment about how he feels his life is going to be after the baby is born. Just concentrate at the moment on the things that you need him to do for you. Baby shopping, rooms that need to be changed around to suit baby's needs. If there are things that he can practically do, then get him involved. This is his baby, too, and he had just as much involvement in creating it as you did.

Concentrate on getting your home ready and get dad to be involved, especially over the next few weeks.

While you have time now, see if there are any local mum and baby groups close to you that maybe you would like to get involved in. You will be at home with the baby more than your partner and you may want to get out and about and meet other people. If you have family who are willing to come and stay for a bit, see if they are happy to; everyone loves a new baby and all the cuddles.

Look after yourself before baby arrives, get as much rest as possible. Don't get into any serious arguments with your partner over events that may or may not happen in the future. Things may be completely different when the baby arrives, and his priorities will change.

Q. My little lad has just started Montessori school. I took extended leave when he was born, and then a career break as I wanted to be at home with him for the first few years. We've had a fantastic time together, exploring the world around us and it's given me so much joy to see him learning all about nature.

I know it's natural for me to be a bit upset that he is now going off to preschool and I know I'll manage this, the problem is that he is so upset every time I drop him off. He cries when he sees us pulling up to the crèche, and cries the whole way in, and tries to cling to my leg to stop me from leaving. I know this is the best thing for him, but it is so hard to see him get so upset and to know that I am causing this. Have you any advice on how I can make this easier for him and for me?

Anxiety

A. I'm sure there are a number of parents out there listening who are nodding in agreement and thinking back to the exact same time in their lives with young children.

You have just had a wonderful time with your new baby and built up a lovely bond while you have been able to stay at home with him. Feeling upset, anxious, and worried about the next step is only natural for you and for your child. He has really only known you as his closest carer and the person he would seek out first for comfort and love. This new routine is going to take some getting used to—especially for your son—and you will have to learn to take each day and each little step forward it gives you and your son. When you potty trained your son, did he get it straight away and that was that? Did he learn to speak and then know every word? No, and this is no different. It's small steps, give him time and allow him the time to be upset and feel what he is feeling.

I have spoken to crèche workers, and, for them, it's the parents who hang around for too long, keep peering in the window, or take too much time trying to settle their child before they go into their classroom that cause more upset for their child. Crèche staff would recommend that you bring in your child and just drop them off and go, most of the time the child will become distracted by something going on and forget why they were upset in the first place.

Most children's attention span is limited and it doesn't take long for them to be distracted and off playing. You could just try this, as hard as it might be, and then check in with the crèche to see if he's settled.

I'm sure you've done your research in relation to the crèche you have decided to send your child to, and you are happy with the staff and care your child will get. So it's time to trust them; they are all qualified staff, and because they are somewhat removed from the children, they are the best for getting them on with their day and making it fun for them, too. Some parents will get embarrassed about leaving off a child that cries every day, but they are so used to it, it's part of their job and they know how best to look after your child. They are not going to leave them crying in a corner!

Keep going, it will change eventually and if your child is continuing to be upset every day for a very long period of time, the crèche will call you and have a chat about what is going on. This is the next step in your child's development—after this is primary school, then secondary, and then college—so he needs to get used to this routine and it will help him in the long run to deal with more prolonged times away from you.

Maybe it's time to also look at what you might like to do to distract yourself from the fact that your child is moving on and you are missing him. I'm not sure if you are going back to work. If so, what would you like to do, or, if you are returning to an old job, are there changes you would like to make there?

If you are staying home, are there projects you would like to get done or a new interest you would like to start? There are so many possibilities for you and your son now, and you can always make sure that if you are home when he is finished, that you can have a lovely half hour of sitting and cuddling while he tells you about his day.

BEING A PARENT

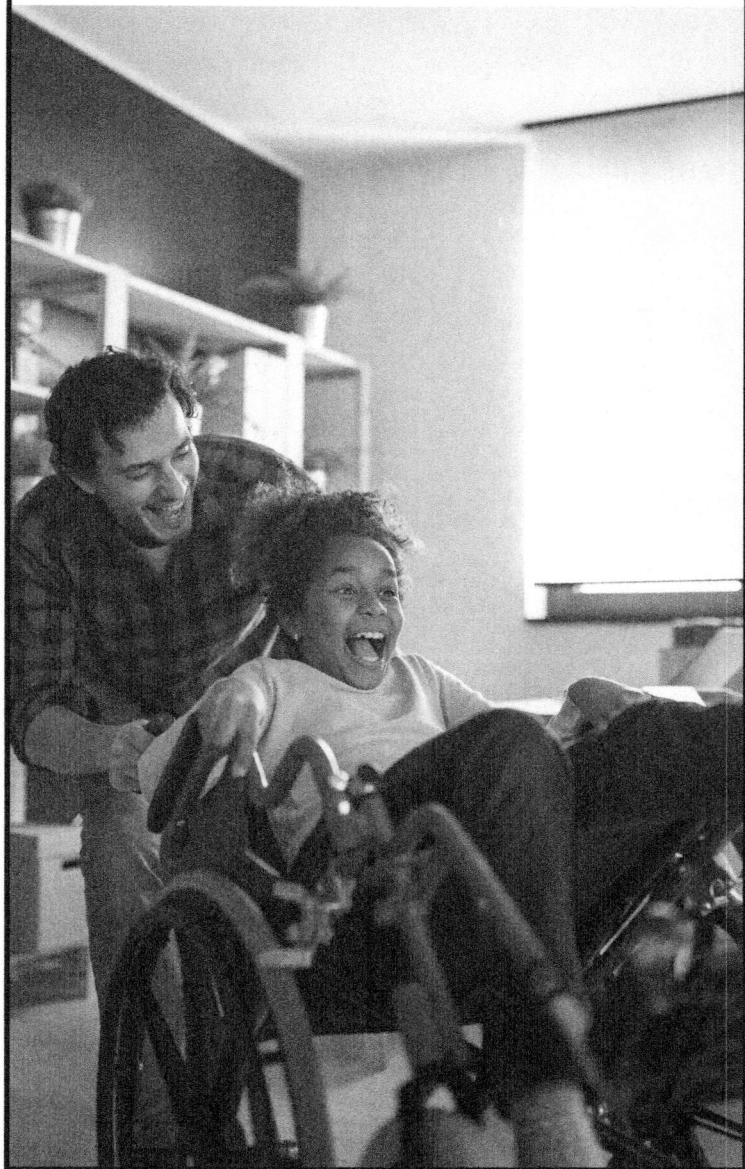

Q. Is it ok to lie to your child? I'm talking about little fibs that parents often tell like, "if you keep picking your nose it'll fall off," and "when the ice cream van plays music it means they've sold out." Are they harmless enough, or is the truth always the best policy? Sometimes it's easier just to make something silly up than sit through an argument or tantrum about something so small. Or even just lies like when your child asks you if fairies or unicorns are real and you say yes because you want them to keep that childhood magic as long as possible.

A. I'm asked this a bit, and as you mention, it is so important to keep childhood magic going for as long as necessary when they are young. Little "white" lies about unicorns and fairies and other childhood magical figures is totally acceptable. I have had parents who would disagree with this and feel children should not be lied to and should be told the truth at all times regardless of what is being discussed.

For children, with young and developing minds, being honest about every story they read or every magical creature they encounter, and dispelling the magic isn't good for them. They are in a lovely stage of their lives where imagination is important, being able to live in make-believe when they are playing by themselves or with others. Their brains need time to develop, to help them deal with all the new experiences they are going through in their lives. They need to be able to switch off the truth of every day life sometimes, especially if they are dealing with something serious in their lives, like a family death or a difficult time in school. As children grow older and their brains develop more and they are having more grown up conversations with their friends they will naturally realise that certain things don't exist, and, yeah, maybe you did lie to them, but they won't hate you for it, and they, in turn, will give their children the opportunity to explore their imagination and see how important it is to have their form of escape.

We need to allow our children to be just that, children. There is so much going on in the world that they do not need to be aware of at a young age, they need some protection. They will be adults for long enough and will be in the real world for a very long time, so let them enjoy this time. If your child turns around to you when they are twenty-two or twenty-three and gives out to you for telling them that their nose will fall off if they keep picking it but it didn't, and you were lying to them all those years, well they have very little to be worrying about!

Q. I quit work while my children were young as I wanted to be there for them in the early years. I was really lucky to be in the position to do that. They've now gotten older where they need me less and I'm starting to get an itch to get back doing something else. I was working in finance, but I don't think I want to do that. My problem is, what do I do? I've no idea where to even start thinking about what I might like to do! Any suggestions?

A. This may resonate with a number of mums who, if financially possible, after having a couple of children, were able to stay at home with them until they started in crèche or school. It's a lovely time with them and a very lucky position to be in.

Your past career was finance and it's not something you want to go back to, but it's what you know, and you could possibly get a job easily enough. When you've had a career break and time to think about the future, it can be daunting to consider retraining or studying again and start a whole new career. You wonder if you have the time to dedicate to the course, or will it be too much as you are still mum to your children and have a home to be involved in, too.

You may need to sit back and have a think about what you would like to do in the future. Years ago, you started your working career in one field, and usually with one company, and you stayed there until retirement.

Nowadays, there are so many more opportunities for people to retrain or go into a different area of their chosen career. You're not tied to the one job, one company, and most companies now expect a certain amount of staff turnover every two to three years.

In my work, I also work with adults in a life coaching capacity and help them to discover what it is they would like to do career wise or help them to steer their life in the direction they really want to go in and enjoy doing.

You may love sitting down and watching soaps on TV, maybe that's your passion. Is this something you could turn into a bigger interest like starting up an online blog or weekly reviews?

There may be something when you were younger that you would have loved to have studied and worked in, but perhaps parents had a decision on your career path. Think back to hobbies and pastimes you were or are still interested in and see are these something you would like to expand on?

Look at the path you will have to take if you choose to change your career. You will need to look for available courses, where are they located and is there a cost involved? Once you have a few that you may be interested in, try and get a taster session done and get in touch with people who have done the course and get feedback from them in terms of what is involved. This is a good idea especially if you are looking at a course that has three or four years of commitment financially and time-wise.

There are loads of online, bite-sized courses that would be available to you if you wanted to explore some possible options. They are usually inexpensive and quick, but will give you an insight into a course that you may like to take up.

Try and take yourself out of the house, away from family and other distractions, and do up a mind map of ideas for courses or possible new careers. Write everything down, all your interests, as something might just jump out at you. Then, if you do see something that interests you, break it down into how you will get to that career and is it practical and realistic and something you could see a future in. If you don't write down what you would like to do, it gets stuck in your head along with all the other day-to-day things you have to do, and it will get lost and possibly forgotten about.

This is a really exciting and important time for you. You have spent a number of years looking after your children to get them to a point where they are more independent, so now it's time for you. It will be great for your children seeing you in a different light and realising that you are a person, too, who has aspirations and desires outside of the family life. Children learn so much more from what they see, and if you are out working or following a dream, they will be experiencing how important it is to have your own time and life outside of family.

Q. My fifteen-year-old son wants to get a tattoo. I have nothing against tattoos and have a few myself, but I have read that children under eighteen, by law, can't get a tattoo. I'm also slow to let him do it as he's still growing, and I don't know how that might impact on his tattoo. What do you think I should do?

A. I am open to correction, but my understanding is that it is illegal for any child under the age of eighteen to get a tattoo, but perhaps check this out for yourself.

Your son is fifteen, and even if he was allowed, you would be hesitant about him doing it. If you are hesitant, why is this? Is it what he is going to get done, or do you not like tattoos? Is your son emotionally ready to get a tattoo, and will he be happy to live with the tattoo he gets done? It's really expensive to get a good, experienced tattoo artist to do a tattoo for you, so make sure that he is going to a reputable artist. If you are in anyway unsure about this, then he needs to wait until he is 18. Three years is very little time to wait, and he will really know if the tattoo is one he wants on his skin for a long time. Is he just getting it done because all his friends are doing it?

Sit down and have a chat with him about the tattoo, what he is getting done. Chat about the tattoo artist he is going to, and check that they are legit. Also discuss the finances for the tattoo and how he is going to pay for it. Let him know that he will have to save up and pay for it himself. The cost of it alone might put him off for a bit!

Q. With the explosion of Christmas Decorations in the shops and advertisements for Christmas all over our TV, my children are driving me nuts to get the decorations up in the house. I don't want to, and I honestly think they won't be able to deal with the length of time if I do put them up. Any suggestions?

A. This happens every year, and it seems as if Christmas is coming earlier and earlier every year. So many companies start their Christmas campaigns as early as the end of October and people start to panic.

This is your house. It's perfectly ok to have the rule that decorations don't go up until the start of December. Explain to your children that you know they are excited, but it's still a long time to the holidays. Start small, get them to start thinking about Christmas lists, letters to Santa, and set a date for early December when you know you have the time available to bring Christmas into the house. Put the decorations up, bake festive treats, and make a day or weekend of it. Sit down in the evenings and watch Christmas movies and enjoy your hard day's work. Your children will see this time at the beginning of December like they do Halloween or Christmas, it's another day to look forward to and get excited about, and they know that the decorations won't come out before that time.

Q. Why is it so difficult to do the same simple morning routine for school? I have three kids who go to school, and every morning there is at least one child who is missing a uniform or a shoe or a tie or hair all over the place. The routine doesn't change, why is it so difficult????

A. Forgetful kids!!! It can be so frustrating when you are trying to get so many bodies out to school and work and the same thing happens nearly every day. If your routine is not working, and you are continuously having the same problems, then maybe it needs to be tweaked a little bit.

Unfortunately, as you are the parent, it will be up to you to look very closely at what happens in the mornings and see where you can change it to help it run more smoothly. Perhaps even getting up 15 minutes earlier might be all it takes to calm things down and get them running more smoothly.

We, as parents, have expectations on how our children should behave and we expect them to act in a more mature way when they are not developmentally at that stage. They need more time to get themselves ready, eat breakfast, and, as children's lives are much busier, and if they are not getting enough sleep at night, they will be even slower. Getting up earlier might help. Give your kids a little check list that they need to go through every morning and they tick the things that they are supposed to look after themselves. Maybe have it in their bedroom so they see it first thing and know what they have to do. This isn't a permanent solution as it will go wrong some mornings, when you sleep in or someone is having a bad morning. If there is one child in particular who makes it harder to get out in the morning, see do they need to get up earlier and help them to get ready. This is a nice time to have a chat with them and discuss the bits and pieces you need them to help you with. It will be a little bit of special time together for both of you.

Q.

I've got an eight-month-old baby...I'm so tired!! How can I freeze time and get some sleep??

A.

Wouldn't it be great if we could get a time freeze machine to catch up on some Zs in those early baby years? There is no way to describe baby tiredness; it is a unique tiredness that feels endless. Have a look at the supports you have around you— i.e. partner, parents, grandparent, aunts and uncles—to see if they can step in anywhere and give you a break a couple of times during the week. Nowadays, a lot of parents feel the pressure to be perfect parents with a perfect home, going back to work, and being able to do it all, but that is very difficult if you are struggling with lack of sleep and a small baby. It's ok for everything in the home not to be perfect and clean and tidy, people don't expect it, especially when you have a baby. It's ok to ask for help, to let people know that you need some sleep as it's having a knock-on effect on everything else in the home. If someone does offer to come in and help out with the baby, make sure you use this time to sleep and not clean or cook or go shopping. Sometimes a good hour of sleep during the day will help you cope a lot better with the rest of the day, and hopefully you can get some help with getting it.

Q. I love my three boys dearly. They're eleven, eight and four. They're so much fun and love just playing around. Obviously, this gets tiring at times, but from talking to my friends, that's just normal for parents. What I struggle with, and no one knows this, is that I feel a real lack of connection with my middle boy. Every day he does something that gets under my skin and in my really low moments, I feel like I just don't like him at all. Even typing this makes me feel so guilty. I try all the time to spend quality time with him and build that relationship, but inevitably he takes something too far and pushes me to the point that I end up having to give out to him. I really feel ashamed that I feel this way, so is there anything I can do to change it?

A. Thank you for your openness and honesty, and I'm sure there are a number of parents reading this who are struggling with something similar. I've worked with clients in the past who have admitted that they don't like their children and struggle sometimes to be a loving and kind parent towards them.

It takes a lot of courage to send this question in; there will be people who will completely understand what you are going through, and then there will be those who will judge—perhaps those who don't or can't have children—and feel you should be grateful for the children you have.

That's all well and good, but this is what is real for you at the moment, and it seems as if you are trying your best not to be too hard on him as you are aware of your feelings and the fact that he does push it too far.

In order for you to try and get past the annoyance of his behavior, you are going to have to try and rewire your brain and feelings when he does something that is a trigger for you. This takes time, consistency, and the willingness to start all over again if there is a slip up. It will be difficult at times, especially as you are mum to two other boys and life is busy.

It will be worth putting the effort in. Start by looking at what the triggers are that you start to see when you are doing something with your son that annoys you. When is the point that it turns from having fun to being frustrated and angry with him over something? There is a good chance your son is looking for attention; it's a busy home and he has two siblings to deal with too. He may also be very aware of what he is doing and is trying to push the boundaries as far as he can, which is exhausting and not fair. It's difficult to keep having to put boundaries in place, especially if you have been doing something fun, then his behavior changes and you have to correct and get annoyed with him. Maybe he is feeling insecure. He is the middle child, and although a lot of people think it's rubbish about where you are in the family, but being in the middle can be lonely. He's not the first born or the baby of the family, so the way he is treated is different whether people are aware of it or not.

You could feel that you have brought your children up in the same way, with the same amount of love, but you could say "I Love You" to all your boys and each of them could get something different out of it. For years parents have said that they love their children equally but this isn't really true. Our children are different and there will be aspects of them that you love, that frustrate you, or just drive you mad, and that's normal.

So, look at your son's behavior when you start to do something with him, is he hyper, are you short on time but you want to do something with him? You may only have twenty minutes to play with him and instead of it being a quick game of cards, he may ask to do something new and you, unfortunately, have to say no to him, which in turn makes him stroppy. This type of behavior would straight away make you reluctant to want to spend time with him and can then feed into previous feelings from another episode you may have had with him. So, explain to him that you only have twenty minutes, you really want to play with him and spend some time with him, and if he doesn't feel it's enough, then explain he will have to wait until later, but you would have loved to play some cards with him. If he agrees to the twenty minutes and starts playing cards, but his behavior changes, he becomes fidgety or isn't playing the game correctly, just be aware of these changes in this behavior and instead of saying anything to him, maybe just get up and go to the toilet and ask him to set another game of cards up. Break it up for yourself too. Don't sit with the behavior that annoys you. Chat to your son and explain to him that sometimes certain bits of his behavior are not acceptable, especially if he wants to play with you. Give him a code word so that when you say it he knows that the behavior he is exhibiting is not ok and he needs to change it. This gives him more of an idea of his behavior and what it is that triggers a reaction from you, so hopefully he will be able to recognize when this is starting to happen and try and change it before it becomes an issue for you. This will, of course, take time, he is a child and his job is to push the boundaries.

Hopefully the behavior will become less and less and you will have to correct him less often and then give yourself a break. It's alright if you are tired and there are so many things going on that you are a bit stressed and get angry. You are trying your best, you are aware of how you are feeling towards your son, and you want to change it, so that's the best start.

Q. Myself and my husband have four kids. The issue isn't so much the kids, but more so us. Between work, driving the kids to activities, we get so little time together. I'm not worried about us splitting up or anything like that, but I miss having time with him, and he's said the same to me. We used to love going out with friends before children arrived, but by the time we get to Saturday night, we're both so shattered, that all we want to do is go to sleep and get ready for the madness the next day. Have you got some ideas as to how we can give attention to our relationship, without looking for babysitters every weekend as that's just not practical?!

A. You have four children; it's completely normal that you would be tired, and sleep is the only thing both of you have on your mind. You obviously work really well together, are aware of how tired and busy the other person is, but you know that you need some couple time in order for you to stay as strong as you are to keep the madness of family life going.

Getting out together doesn't have to mean getting out every weekend, or when you do go out, going on the rip and then dying for the next three days. Simple things like the movies, lunch out together, and, of course, getting away for a night or two, are all things you could do once a month, or even every couple of months. Sit down and try and have a chat about a plan you would like to put in place in order to be able to get out more regularly together and bring back you as a couple and not just as parents. See who are the people in your lives who would take the children for a night or two—even look at being able to split the children up so it's not being put on one set of grandparents or relatives. If you manage to get a night or two away, it will make the world of difference to you and will help to get on with the busy family life.

See are there times in the day during the week if you can grab a cuppa together or go for a walk when the kids are at activities or in school. Your relationship is obviously really important to you, and sometimes putting the effort in to organize a night out or a trip away will really be worth it in the long run for you as a couple and your family.

Q. I have two children, an eight-year-old girl and a six-year-old boy. I feel that they are completely running the house. I have no control over anything and they never listen to me. I'm completely at the

end of my tether, please help!

A. I get quite a few of these short-but-to-the-point questions looking for some advice and help. This mum has two children who are controlling the home and the balance has been lost. Control seems like a strong word, especially to be using around your children, but it's not controlling your children, it's being able to manage the home, and they need to be respectful of mum and the home. Children are children, growing, learning, and pushing boundaries every day to see what they can get away with before a consequence comes into place.

When you are in this mindset, you need to sit back, not react to every little thing the children do, and work out a plan so you can start to take back control in the home.

Firstly, do you have a partner or husband who can help you to sort this issue out? It's not only yours to try and solve. If you don't have someone in the home with you, do you have a close family member who can help you out? You have so many things going on in your head in terms of the daily upkeep of the home, and trying to get everyone ready for the day ahead. Just trying to deal with these issues is exhausting, never mind also having to try and parent your children who are doing what they want whenever they want. Even if the other person is just there to let you get ideas out or talk about the struggles, this itself can bring about answers and help you to come up with possible solutions.

Try and get out of the house and get some time where you can sit and have a cuppa and work through a parenting plan, how you can break down the parts of your family life that aren't working at the moment. List what it is the children are doing or not doing that is causing the problems. Are they going to school, are they getting up in the morning, are they going to bed on time, are they eating properly? If they are going to school then that's an issue you don't have to worry about, if it's difficult to get them there (i.e. out of bed and have breakfast), then maybe this is something you need to correct. Having an angry house first thing in the morning is exceptionally draining and can snowball as the day goes on.

Do you need to look at their bedtimes, do they get enough sleep? If they don't get enough sleep this can have the knock-on effect of the morning time being really difficult. Are you getting up early enough in the morning so everyone can have breakfast and have enough time to wake up properly? Can you make sure that all the things needed to get out the door in time for school are done the night before (e.g. lunches made, uniforms ready, bags packed)?

If they are doing a number of these things without you having to have an argument with them then that's great and you have a lot more control and management in the home than you realise. Sometimes it can seem as if everything is going wrong especially if you are tired, busy, and there has been no break recently. You are probably doing so much better than you think and this could be one of those ruts that all families find themselves in.

The important thing is to be able to separate the good from the bad and try and pinpoint exactly what it is that's causing the main problems and then figure out how to correct it whether it means bringing in consequences or talking to your children about what is going on. If there is certain every-day behavior that the children are doing, then you need to bring in a consequence and stick to it. Make it relevant to the problem you need corrected. If it's a case of them not picking up after themselves, especially in the evenings, then you can bring in a consequence that they can't watch their favourite tv programme that evening. If it's the same the next day, then it's two days they can't watch the tv, eventually they will see that you are not going to back down and a boundary will be put in place. There is no point in giving them a long consequence for a small issue as they will just push back and possibly be even more of a handful. Try and set out appropriate consequences, get your partner or a family member to help you out, and hopefully in a couple of weeks there will be a bit more order and calm in the home.

Q. We are looking to put our son into a crèche as I am due to go back to work in a month's time. I've loved spending so much time with my son and have built up a huge bond with him. The thoughts of going back to work are keeping me awake as I don't really want to go back, but the biggest issue is childcare. We have no family around locally, and we're finding it extremely difficult to find somewhere that we can get him into and that doesn't cost a mortgage! Have you any suggestions as to what we might do?

A. You've just had this wonderful bonding time with your child; it's incredibly important to have this with your child in their early months. It looks as if a number of companies worldwide are realizing this, too, and are offering longer maternity leave and also extra paternity leave at this really special time.

Can you find a crèche? Is there one locally to you that you can get a place for your child? The emotional side of going back to work after having had a baby and having had a lovely time with him is really difficult and can take a lot of getting used to. A lot of parents would worry about the child and how this new separation will affect them, but I wouldn't worry too much about your child. At this young age, children adapt very quickly, and as long as they are happy and feel safe with whoever is looking after them, they will be ok.

The bigger question here is, are you ok with sending your son to a crèche? You have to go back to work, you don't have family close by to look after your child, so a crèche seems to be the only possible option. Another big question you have to ask yourself is, is it worth going back to work, especially full time? I know the first response to this will be that you need to go back for financial reasons, you couldn't afford to only live on one wage. So there are a couple of things—it's amazing how much money we can save and outgoings that we can cut back on when we do a little bit of work. Utilities and insurances are always the biggest areas we can save on if we haven't changed company in a while, and although it can be a pain having to ring around, the savings could be substantial to your family. If you can cut back on your outgoings and try and be a bit more savvy with the money you do have, you may be able to keep going without having to go back to work. You need to weigh up the cost of crèche, the cost of traveling every day to work,

Being A Parent

and the other money that goes towards work-life (i.e. lunches). If there is little left in your wages after paying out for all of this, you need to seriously consider the possibility of not going back if that is what you would like, or possibly finding a part-time job closer to home, especially if you would like to still have that work experience. If you feel that you will be extra stressed trying to work every day and then have a small amount of time with your child in the evenings, this is something you really need to give some thought to.

The idea of cutting away from work and the income you have coming in is extremely scary. You may have a large mortgage, a lot of bills to pay, and not working is not an option at the moment. That's perfectly understandable, but if you feel your quality of life and that of your family is going to suffer because you are under extra stress of work, then do give this some serious thought.

If, on the other hand, you are going back to work and you need a crèche, then start having a look at the crèches locally and see do you get a good feeling about any of them. If there isn't a space available straight away, can you possibly take some extra time off until one is available? Have you considered a child-minder? There are a lot of qualified people who don't work in crèches but prefer to work from their own home or go to your house to look after your child.

DEALING WITH CONFLICT

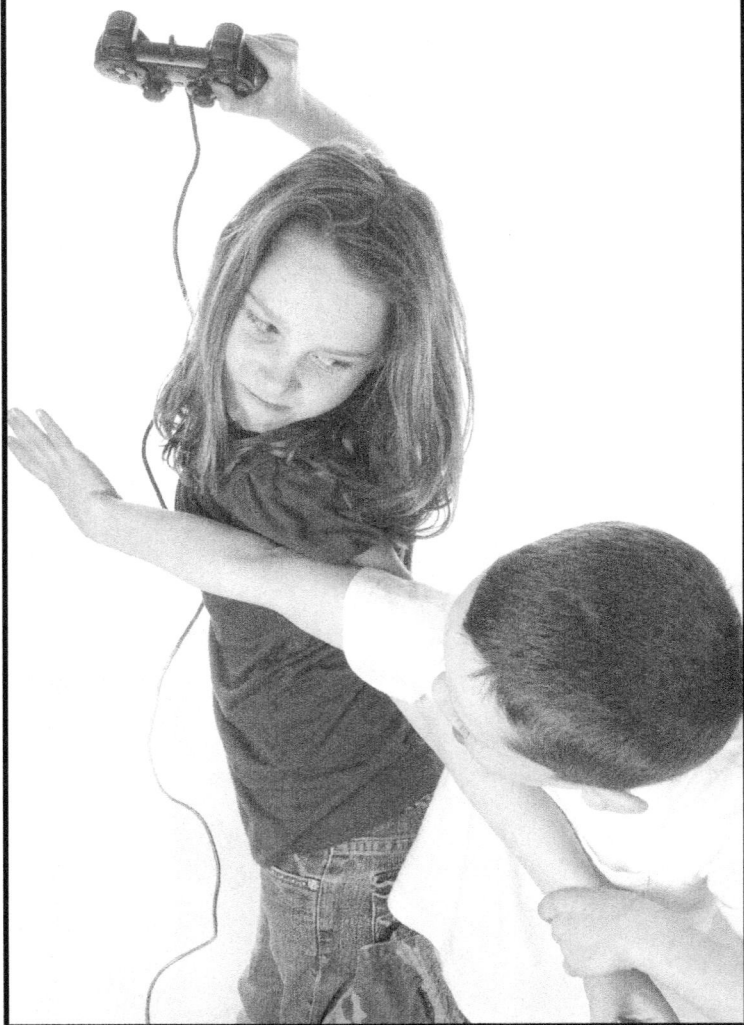

Q. My twin boys are addicted to their PlayStation®. Every day there is an argument to get them to do homework and then come down for dinner. They get really aggressive after playing online with friends. What can we do to stop this?

A. From what you have told me in regards to your sons playing their PlayStation® or another device, it seems as if over-use of them is causing their behaviour to change for the worse. You will need to step in and take serious action to resolve this issue. This will include no use of the devices during the week, especially if it is affecting their ability to do their homework and do simple tasks when asked. If there are arguments over this decision you will need to stand firm and not give in to their whinging and moaning. Make it clear to them that the longer they protest, the longer the confiscation of their devices. It will change, but it will take time and a lot of patience on your part.

Device use will be limited to the weekends, and with a set time limit, so as they don't get to the point where they are fighting, or their behaviour is changing.

All of these restrictions will, of course, be lifted, but your sons need to show responsibility in terms of their device use, and when you do go back to letting them have game time, you will need to set time limits regardless of how well they have been behaving.

You can also look at taking the games they play offline, which will limit their contact with other people, people you don't know, and friends, too. They might turn around to you when they are in their 20s and say you were awful parents for not letting them play games online with their friends. If this is the worst thing you could do to them, then that's ok, and you can apologise to them for it!!!

Have a look at what they are playing; are they age appropriate, violent, and not suitable? Playing games that are not appropriate for their age means your child is frequently dealing with content that they have no experience with, or is too adult for their brains to be able to dissect.

You can't blame your children and their aggression if you are allowing them to play violent games for an unlimited time.

Make sure you and your partner are both on board about the device use, so that your children can't play one off the other. Set the rules, stick to them, but make sure that if there is improvement, then the restrictions can be looked at. Your children also need to know that if they do improve and try to change their behaviour, then they will be treated fairly.

Q. Myself and my wife have two young children, a four-year-old boy and seven-year-old girl. They're good kids and we have a really good relationship. My worry is that my wife won't leave the kids overnight with anyone. We have good family who love the kids and would really like to have them sleep over, but my wife just refuses. I've tried to book nights away for us and even got her a trip to New York for her birthday, but she says the only way she'll go is if the kids come, too. I know this sounds so small, but it impacts our lives as we never go to friends' weddings or events where we would have to stay overnight. I don't want to push her, but when I try to bring it, up she just fobs me off. Any advice?

A. Since I've had children and been in situations like the above with friends who are new parents, I have definitely noticed this behavior more. There is a feeling of needing to be with your children all the time in case something happens, they become upset or sick, and you're not there to help them. It's doesn't have anything to do with family members and not doing good enough a job, it's a fear of upsetting your child and the possibility that they may never get over this and be affected by it for life. Not spending time apart from your children, especially when you know they are safe and being looked after, is not good for anyone. Children need to learn to be away from their parents for long periods of time, especially as they get closer to playschool and primary school age. The likelihood that anything bad will happen to them while you are away is very slim and they will be having lovely experiences with other family members like grandparents,

Dealing with Conflict

aunts and uncles, and forming these bonds with these family members is really important, too. Your family would never let anything bad happen to your children, they will have a great time with them, and then there will be the excitement of seeing you again when you come to pick them up. You can sit down with them and listen to all the adventures that they had, you can tell them about your time away, and you can look forward to the next sleepover they have.

At some point, your children will have to be away from you and your wife for a period of time. Life is like that, and it is impossible to plan every waking moment of your life and not have any emergencies or events that take a different turn.

The worst case scenario is very unlikely to happen, it's nearly always the opposite, so you need to try and get your wife to look at the positives of your children having time away from you and being with other relatives, and, also, how important it is to you as a couple to have time alone together. You didn't meet as parents, you met as a couple, and your relationship has now evolved to being a family. But it if wasn't for the bond you made in the first place, you wouldn't be together now, so it's really important to look after that relationship, too. There is no taking away from the fact that you are parents, you always will be, but there is no reason why you can't have a bit of time for yourselves, too.

As your children grow and experience playschool, primary school, and college, they need to be able to learn to be away from you and become more independent. You don't have children in order to keep them at home and not experience life. Your job is to look after them, nurture them, and prepare them for independent living when they leave school or college and go off to work, so that they can do the same for their families, if and when they have them.

There are a lot more cases of anxiety among children, and a certain amount of this can come from parents and their anxiety. Children are very aware of atmospheres and feelings that go on with their parents, and although they may not be able to verbalize what it is, this can come out in them through anxiety. In order for our children to feel safe and secure, we need to let them go and be happy about the progress they are making in life on their own.

Perhaps try and have a conversation with your partner over dinner one evening when the kids are in bed, and let them know that you understand how they're feeling. Let her know that you love her, that your relationship with her is really important, and that you would like to be able to have time for just the two of you, which would include going away. Let her know that the children will be ok with whoever they are left with and that's it's really important that they get time away from you, the parents, too.

If you feel that she's really struggling to leave the children, and her anxiety is affecting other parts of her life, she may need to go and chat to someone, perhaps her GP or a counsellor. You are coming from a caring place with concern for your wife and your children, so hopefully she will see this and you can have a conversation about how you can change this situation.

Q. My twelve-year-old and my seven-year-old were having an argument recently, and in the heat of the fight, my eldest boy told the youngest that there was no Easter Bunny. I now have a devastated seven-year-old and very remorseful twelve-year-old. How do I sort this mess out?

A. Unfortunately, when arguments happen, more than likely things will be said that we don't mean or should never have said in the first place. We feel remorseful and bad about the words we used, whether they are true or not, and it's not different for your children.

Your twelve-year-old is now feeling awful for saying what they did and wishes they can take it back. Quite possibly your twelve-year-old was provoked, especially if they were both fighting, but that doesn't excuse what they did and amends need to be made.

So, children fight and you have to reprimand them and try and not let it happen too often. You can sit down with your children and let them know that the fighting behavior is not ok, so that they don't get to the point when things are said and feelings are hurt. The onus should not just be on the older child either, your younger child needs to learn when enough is enough and take responsibility for their actions too.

Now, back to the issue of the Easter Bunny. You will need to sit down with your older child and let them know that what they did was wrong, although this may not be necessary as I'm sure they are feeling bad enough about it already. Next, they will need to go to their younger sibling and let them know that they were lying when they said there is no such thing as the Easter Bunny. Let them know that you said it because you were angry and wanted to hurt them, which wasn't ok. This will help your older child to realise what they did, and what it takes to try and make things better. It would be a good idea to be close at hand when this is happening, so that another fight doesn't happen, just in case. Your younger child may then come to you to look for reassurance that there is an Easter Bunny, and this is when you let them know there is, and hopefully this will be enough for the issues to be resolved.

Q. My twin boys are eleven and are constantly killing each other. I've tried lots of different things to get them to stop but nothing seems to work. I'm at the end of my tether with them, and I find myself almost getting dragged into the middle of arguments, and I end up feeling terrible, and they just get on with things. Any suggestions as to what to do?

A. So, going on the information you have given me, it seems as if you may need to look at the consequences you have in place if your boys step out of line. It may be that what you have in place at the moment is too lenient and may need adjusting, so that it is enough for your sons to see that you are serious about them changing their behavior. And unless this starts to happen, then the consequences will be kept in place. Look at consequences that have worked well in the past and perhaps look at using them again. Try and sort this out as soon as you can. With a lot of situations like this, there is a cycle of conflict. The first thing is: what has caused the conflict in the first place (i.e. your kids never make their bed and I get frustrated)? Next, something happens like they don't make their beds again, and then an argument follows, and then you have to look at the resolution to get what you need done.

Firstly, sit down with your sons and have a chat about the behavior and how it is not acceptable. When you are stressed, you find it very difficult to let things go, and the smallest thing can set you off. The stress trigger here for you is the boys fighting and you don't want to get dragged into it and for it to become an even bigger issue. Let them know that their fighting makes you feel stressed. You can show them the circle of conflict, it's on Google. You'll show them and let them start to take some responsibility for their actions. They may only be eleven, but they are old enough to take responsibility for their actions.

Start a conversation around what it is that annoys the other twin, starts an argument, and leads to the fighting. Put the responsibility on them to stop the fighting and learn to ignore each other. If this doesn't work, then the consequences need to come in. This could be not being allowed to go to a party, or less time on tv or a device. You will need to stick to these consequences for the time period you have installed, even when it's really difficult and you just want to cave in because they are annoying you about it.

Have a look at your own stress levels. Are you feeling overwhelmed in work, at home or just with the boys? Do you need some extra support, need to speak to someone outside of everything? Life with two eleven-year-old boys must be really hectic at times, so you need to make sure you are doing ok, too, so you can deal with their antics.

EDUCATION &
EXAMS

Q. Myself and my husband are disagreeing a lot over where to send our son to school. He is due to start primary school next September and I really want to send him to a school with a strong history of successful students, while my husband wants to send him to the local school with his friends. Have you any advice on how we can resolve this issue?

A. For a lot of parents this is something that wouldn't be a discussion, it would be the closest school with their pals like they probably did themselves. But for a couple who may have different ideas on how they would like their child to be educated, this can be a tough situation to get through and agree on. We all want a good education for our child and the majority of schools nowadays provide just that with excellent teachers and supports in place if needed. We all want the school where our child is happy to go there every day, has lovely experiences, gets a great education, and finishes feeling happy and ready for the next stage of their education.

It is impossible for any parent to know what is going to work best for their child/children. Parents may feel that sending their child to the local school with friends will give them a happier start as they will know other children and will enjoy the whole process better. They may feel that if their child is happy going, they will be more open to learning and do well in school.

Other parents may believe the best education is one that is paid for as the class number may be smaller, the school can offer a wider variety of learning for their child, and they will have better experiences in a paid education.

Neither of the above options are right or wrong; no one knows how a child will settle into education, how they will learn, or what they may struggle with.

Some parents will decide based on how they were educated and what their parents wanted for them in terms of prospects for the future (i.e. good job, success). This can create a lot of pressure on a child from a very early age.

In a lot of schools, the emphasis has changed somewhat in terms of what is really important to get out of a school education. There is more done in terms of practical lessons that are needed to get you through life like dealing with anxiety, pressure, being aware of your wellbeing, and not just the materialistic elements of life.

It is about trying to get a balance for you and your child. You may send your child to the school that has great academic records, but this could result in pressure for your child if they are struggling to learn or present with a learning disability like dyslexia in a later school year. There may not be supports in place in this school to help them and you may need to change schools.

People go through so many different careers in a lifetime, and getting a good base education is great, support from parents is really important, and encouragement in whatever career path they choose to take is paramount.

You will need to sit down together and ask yourselves what it is you want for your child long-term: good job, loads of money, happiness and fulfillment in whatever they do?

Your child is young, it is primary school, and there needs to be an element of fun at this age too. You have a lot to think about and discuss in terms of what is most important about your child's education.

There can be no blame put on the parent if the school you do send your child to doesn't work out—you made a decision together and you will need to tackle it together, too, for the best interests of your child.

Q. My daughter is in first year in school and has adapted really well to the new school. She's doing really well in most of her subjects, but we're beginning to see a bit of a pattern where, with subjects she's not keen on or finds a bit more difficult, she is struggling to take in the information, which has resulted in her getting anxious about simple class tests. We understand the fact that she may not be too bothered with some subjects, but the reality is she has to do them, and we don't want her getting behind in the work as this will only add to her stress levels. Have you any ideas on how we can manage this?

A. We all have subjects in school that we find boring—mind-numbingly boring—and that's ok. Unfortunately with school, we can't just do the subjects we love, we also have to do the ones we're not too keen on too. It's important that you don't allow your child to underperform in a certain subject just because they don't like it or find it boring. You may need to look at how your child works best, and it may be that you all get on board to help your child work through this subject. I have a multiple intelligences test that your child could take and this may give you a better idea on how to help them study and learn in this subject.

Look at what it is about the subject that they don't like. Is it the teacher, is it a certain topic they are studying at the moment? You are right, you don't want your child falling behind in a subject now as in a couple of years' time it will be more difficult to make up for the lost study, especially when they may be trying to study for state exams. You may need to put some extra time into the subjects your child doesn't enjoy, especially if she is happily working along in her other subjects.

After a while she will just do it automatically, perhaps not enjoy it, but just do it anyway. It's perfectly ok to accept and agree with your daughter in terms of not liking the subject as that's normal, but she needs to know that like all the subjects she does enjoy, she still needs to do the work on the ones she doesn't like. So help each other out, try not to get too focused on it, and put a little bit more time towards subjects she's not enjoying. Hopefully it won't take long for her to accept that they need to be done and will just do it!

Q. My daughter is having to make her school subject options and came home saying she no longer wanted to do Home Economics, which had been her first choice all along, as another student told her it was hard, and she wanted to pick a subject that she has never shown any interest in because she was told it was easy. She loves baking and learning about things like that. How can we get her to choose the subject we know that she'll love and do really well in?

A. In Ireland when a child is in first year of secondary school, they need to make a decision on certain subjects that they would like to do for the rest of their school time.

It's a good idea to sit down and talk to your child about their decisions. Have a conversation with them that they are not getting an overall view of a subject based on one person's experience and the fact that they found it difficult. That's not necessarily how it will work out for them and perhaps they could speak to other students who are taking that subject. There is a good chance that if your daughter enjoys elements of a subject outside of school time, they will more than likely enjoy the subject, and it may not be as difficult for them as it was for the student who said it was difficult.

Chat about the fact that she is good at many of the elements that will be involved in Home Economics. Make sure she has a good think about why she now doesn't want to do this subject and perhaps do a subject that she thinks may be easy based on someone else's experience.

Whatever subject she does choose will need hard work and study and sometimes if you do a subject that you are interested in, that work doesn't seem so difficult as you are enjoying the topics as you go along.

You may need to put your foot down, even if these are her choices especially if her reasons are not good enough. She can hate you later if it doesn't work out for her!!

Q. Our nine-year-old has not been a big fan of attending school this year, especially since they've been back after winter break. She goes willingly, but is grumpy about how she wishes it was a stay-home day, or wishes she could be home to spend time with friends. Her best friends in our neighborhood are a year or two older and attend different schools. Regardless, we want our daughter to like school and feel motivated, and it feels like such a struggle right now. Any advice on how we can help get her to be a bit more positive about school?

A. Like a previous question, this is a want that you have for your child and not how she is feeling at the moment. She may really dislike school, a lot of children do even if it is the most state of the art, fun place to be. It's not for everyone. I don't have very fond memories of school. It wasn't all bad, but I didn't enjoy having to sit at my desk all day and learn things that I had no interest in.

Your daughter may not be overly motivated about school; it could be something outside learning hours that really makes her happy (i.e. her friends). She is becoming more aware of herself as an individual, her voice, and her likes and dislikes. She's also just finished her holidays, loads of fun, time to herself, and with her friends, so it's difficult to get back into the routine of up early, hours of school, and homework.

You mention that this whole school year has been tedious for you. It's been difficult to motivate her to go to school and like it. Unfortunately, it may just be a phase you will have to work through with her, but that doesn't mean that you have to put up with continuous complaining, moaning, and bad behaviour because she doesn't want to go to school. It's compulsory and she needs to do it. You can explain this to her and put consequences in place if she continues behaving this way.

Let her know you understand, school isn't for everyone, but she isn't making it any easier on herself or the family if she is complaining all the time, so put a consequence in place and see if this helps.

Q. My thirteen-year-old daughter is fairly conscientious and gets her homework done and we help her when she needs it. One of her good friends in school has been asking a lot for her to send her my daughter's homework as she doesn't understand what to do. It wasn't a big deal to start, but now it's clear that her friend is taking advantage. My daughter doesn't see it as a big issue, but it's something we don't want to continue, as our daughter may get in trouble in school. Any advice on how to handle it?

A. If this is your child's first year in secondary school, they are probably just starting to make new friendships and learning to know about new people in their class. If she is conscientious, she probably has no problem sending on the homework to the friend, especially if she has it done, it's not an issue for her.

Sometimes this can be a nice sign, she's obviously being really nice and other people see it and she can be relied upon to help out if needed.

At the same time, you don't want to see her getting taken advantage of, especially if it is happening every night and she is getting messages late into the evening when she is going to bed or sitting down and relaxing.

It could be that her friend is struggling to get used to all the new subjects and keeping track of what she has to do, and because your daughter is so helpful, she is turning to her, but you need to let your daughter know that it's ok to say no and to use you as an excuse as to why she can't send on the homework all the time. Take the onus off your daughter, step in, and help her to help her friend.

Her friend will need to learn the tools to become more organised and remember to take down the homework and then complete it herself. Perhaps this is something she needs to bring up with her parents especially if she is struggling to cope. She may start to fall behind and not understand the subjects and this becomes a bigger issue for the friend.

Let your daughter know that you will take the blame as to why she can't share her homework anymore. Offer help, do homework together if possible. It sounds as if this is the start of a really good friendship, and good friends help each other, but they also are there to pull you up on things, too.

If it continues, and your daughter keeps sending the homework, then you may need to make a call to her friend's parents and talk it through.

Q. I left school when I was thirteen and never went back, it just wasn't for me. The problem I'm having now is that my ten-year-old has started coming home with homework, and some of it, I just don't understand. I don't want my child thinking I'm stupid, but I don't want to be giving her the wrong way to do something or the wrong answers. How do you think I can deal with this without feeling like I'm stupid, just like I did in school?

A. When we have a negative association with something like school, and then our children start their school years, the feelings you may not have had in many years can start to resurface. And in your case, they aren't good memories. You may start to feel stupid, think about how the teachers made you feel, and have concerns for your own children. No one wants to feel stupid, and that's normal. You could sit down with your child and let them know that you've forgotten how to do some of the school work because it's been so long, but you could sit down together and look up solutions. Doing this allows you to refresh or learn new skills that will help your child with their school work and, more than likely, you will have developed your own way of working out things, and these methods could be a useful way of helping.

If this is something that is really worrying you, could you go back to education and do your leaving certificate? It will be a very different learning experience for you now you are an adult and not being forced to do the work. You never know, it could open the door to continued learning in a subject that really interests you and could lead to employment.

If you are comfortable with the teachers in your child's school and happy to talk to them, they have loads of resources to help parents with children's school work. The curriculum has changed so much over the years, and many of the methods used when we were learning have changed significantly, even the most educated of people would struggle nowadays.

It's ok to let your children know that you can't figure out their math or English homework, it's normal. You can have fun figuring it out together.

Start to look at local resources in your library or adult education centre, they will have loads tools to help and you will meet people in similar situations.

Q. My son has just finished the Leaving Cert and, to me, didn't appear to do much work or put in much effort for his exams. We've had a large amount of arguments about this, and the tension throughout the year in the house has been unbearable at times. I tried to get him to study during the year, and all he would say to me was, "I am studying, Mam, you're just adding more pressure to me." This frustrated the hell out of me. I was only trying to support him as I know he has so much potential.

The exams are over now and things have relaxed a bit in the house, but I can't help but worry that he won't get into college and that he'll end up in some crappy job with no future prospects. He's such a clever lad, but just doesn't apply himself. He's heading off on holidays with his friends, which we are paying for, and has no job lined up for when he gets back. I hate seeing him lounge around and really don't want to see that this summer. How can I get him to realise that we can't keep paying for his lifestyle, and he needs to start pulling his weight and take responsibility for his life?

A. There is a lot going on here. We'll break it up into parts. One of the biggest events in a child's life that will bring about a number of stressful situations and arguments in the home will be exams and study, especially significant final exams. As parents we look at our children and how much time they are spending in their rooms studying—they could be in there for two or three hours but not necessarily studying! In the majority of cases of children studying in their rooms for long periods of time, they will start to lose interest in the subject about 45 minutes in and will become distracted. This is normal teenage behavior and is the case for most adults, too. We only have a certain amount of time that we are truly focused on something before we start thinking of other things. It's also the reason why most classes in school are only forty-five minutes long as children will become bored and restless after this time.

If we were to see our children coming downstairs after only forty-five minutes of study we would start to question them and what they are doing as they haven't been at it for very long. But if they've been up there and truly studying for that length of time, then it's time for them to take a fifteen-minute break, have a snack, glass of water, or just sit on their phones for a few minutes.

All children study in different ways and take information in using different techniques. Some people need a distraction like music or be able to move around the room as they learn subjects.

There is a good chance that your son did do enough studying for his exams and will get into college. You will need to just put the worry aside until the results come out as your stress isn't going to change the outcome.

Now that the summer has arrived and he's looking forward to having a bit of downtime after the exams, you need to let him enjoy the bit of freedom, but before he goes, he needs to commit to getting a job when he gets back. It doesn't really matter what the job is or how well it pays, this has got to do with setting up a routine for him before the results come out and he is looking at possible college options for September/October.

You need to let him know that you are paying for the holiday, but that the bank of mum and dad won't be supporting him all summer, and as he is an adult, he needs to be providing for himself. You're not necessarily asking him to contribute to the family household budget, but you will be expecting him to be able to pay for his own fun, clothes. This will be a really good way to get used to having to pay for his own way, especially if he goes off to college. He may need to get a job to supplement his college money and will need to learn to budget and make his money last.

You might be surprised, he may sort a job out before he goes on holidays, he might be really positive when he gets back from his holidays and start looking straight away, or he may try and chance not getting a job. You will need to stand firm on this situation as it will be of great benefit to him in the long run.

The last part of your question. What if he doesn't get into college? So, the normal progression for school-going children nowadays is college, especially as most jobs now require at least a basic college qualification.

Of course, this isn't the path that works for everyone, and it may take a little longer for your son to get a college degree, especially if he's not sure what he would like to do.

There are many different avenues that children now take in order to get to their chosen career and some people don't go to college at all. There are apprentices, community college courses, work that leads to a forever job, and there is college. If your son isn't ready to make a decision on what he would like to do, then perhaps he could enroll in a one-year course in an area that he is somewhat interested in, while also having a part-time job to supplement the money you give him. Many job careers take different turns over the years; think of where you started out yourself. It's really important that your son does enroll in something after the results come out, or if not, he looks for a more permanent job or repeats his exams. It may be a tough time, but it will settle. Try to be as supportive as possible in his decisions but make sure he's not sitting around doing nothing. Get involved, let him know you are there for him, and help him as well as you possibly can with this next part of his adult life.

FAMILY

Q. My sister and her partner every Christmas go crazy buying gifts for everyone and end up putting themselves in a ton of debt each year. I've tried talking to her about it but she just blows it off. The issue I have is that my kids are becoming more aware of the significant difference between what they get and what their cousins get. Is there any thing I can do to manage this better as its stressing me out.

A. This is tough. Obviously your sister is not worried about going into debt at Christmas, and if that is the case, then realistically there is nothing you can do about it. She is an adult and that is her family and her financial situation to deal with.

You can have a chat with your children about what they receive at Christmas. Explain to them that Santa only delivers so many presents to each household and we should be really grateful for what you do receive as we are really lucky. There will always be people who get more, are better at something, are more popular, but it's important to teach your children to be happy with what they have and be grateful for it. It's a good time to show them families and children that are not that well off and received little or nothing at Christmas. It will show them how lucky they are, and it's great to help raise a bit of money or donate to a children's charity.

Maybe you could talk to the whole family and suggest Kris Kringle for the children, where each couple takes one or two children and buys a gift for them instead of buying presents for all the nieces and nephews. Perhaps suggest not buying presents for the adults. Most adults have all they need, and if they don't, they can buy it themselves, or suggest Kris Kringle for them too.

There are fewer presents, but they are appreciated a lot more. Your children will be ok with fewer gifts; they are still going to get what they would like, and they will learn that there are limits, and it will teach them good lessons for the future.

Sometimes we need to not give in to the outside pressures and just concentrate on our own little families and how it works best for all of you.

Q. I have four children under the age of nine and I rely heavily on my parents to help bring them up as I am a single parent and work part time. The issue is that they constantly undermine me in front of my children, which means that when I get home with the kids, they are much harder to manage. I don't want to hurt my parents' feelings, but I can't keep going like this as it is bringing me down, and I end up with a very short fuse with the kids. What can I do to make them understand?

A. Grandparents minding grandchildren regularly so their children can work has become increasingly common in a lot of households. Your parents don't want to see you have to spend large amounts of money on childcare, want to spend time with their grandchildren, and help as much as possible, but sometimes it's not the best solution. Your children are your children and you have chosen to bring them up in certain manner. Your parents did it their way, and although they are doing you a huge favor, that doesn't give them the right to undermine you. I'm sure when they first started, you gave them a routine to follow, information on behavior, but at the same time you would be aware that they've already done all this. They need to be respectful of the fact that they are helping with your children, not their own, and it's now causing you stress and anxiety and it's not fair to take it out on the children.

It's going to take courage to sit down and have a chat with them. If possible, try and write down exactly what you want to say, then read it back and make a list of real issues that need to discussed. This isn't a list of things they are doing wrong, it's to help everyone, so that the situation doesn't get worse and you end up with a strained relationship with your parents. If you can't face them, then write a letter and give it to them. If they understand, there will be no problems and if they can't see the problem, then unfortunately you may need to reconsider your parents looking after your children, which won't be ideal. If your partner can help out, get them involved, too. They are his responsibility also, and this is a really tough situation to be in.

Q. With Easter coming, I'm really worried about the amount of chocolate my three kids get. Every year the house is falling down with eggs and I don't want them eating it all. Another issue is that myself and my husband end up eating a lot of it, and neither of us want that either. How do I stop people buying my children eggs?

A. Most parents will experience this happening when they have young children and Easter comes around. You are trying to keep your children healthy by limiting what they eat, but you then end up eating even more yourself, and that's not good either.

We've had ten or twelve Easter eggs for one child in our home, and it's crazy, too much chocolate, too much waste. It's lovely that friends and family gift your children the eggs, as it's their way of showing their love, but when it's more than two, it's harder to deal with.

There are, of course, ways to deal with this, so that your children and you enjoy Easter and all the chocolate goodness that comes with it. As parents are becoming more aware of how much chocolate their children consume, they've needed to become more clever at dealing with the excess, and that doesn't just mean eating it themselves or throwing it out.

You are, of course, going to let your children have some chocolate over the holidays, so if you feel that two eggs is enough for each child then let them pick the ones that would like to keep and let them enjoy every mouthful.

Possible solutions I've heard for the rest of the eggs have been to donate the eggs to a local charity, homeless aid, or women's refuge. They are always happy to receive donations even if it is a little bit past the actual day.

Hold a cake sale for charity and invite people around. This way you use up the chocolate, it's spread out among more people, and you raise some money for a local charity.

The hardest one to do in order to change the habit of family and friends is to ask them not to give so much chocolate. Let them know that you are trying to keep the children and yourselves healthy, and that a book or an item of clothing would be greatly appreciated instead of chocolate. Some relatives may ignore the request, and if this is the case, just say 'thanks' and use one of the possible solutions mentioned above.

There are loads of ways of stopping your children and yourselves from eating too much. It also allows you to bring up topics with your children around those who don't have enough and why it would be good to donate the eggs to families that need it more. Gets them thinking about others and lets them realise how lucky they are to have all that they have themselves.

KIDS'
QUESTIONS

Q.

Why do parents always tell you to get off electronics and go outside?

A.

Our kids learn more from what they see than what they hear! If we are having to tell them to get off their devices and go outside, then maybe we, the adults, need to do the same!

Your parents are just trying to keep you healthy and happy, so it's important not to be on your devices for too long. I've seen it happen where a child is on a device for too long and they become angry and switched off from everything else, and they take it out on family and it takes a long time for them to calm down.

Go along with it, don't complain, and get some fresh air. Parents, if you are on your device too much, you need to do the same. And if it's raining, well, that's why raincoats were invented!!!

Q.

Why do parents make you have showers?

A.

The reasons parents make you have showers is because if you don't, you will smell, which isn't good for anyone! It's important to keep your skin clean especially if you are regularly doing sports. Being smelly is not nice to be around. Friends may not want to be around you and your parents may consider setting you up outside with the dog. Have a wash—it's quick, it makes you feel awake and you will smell nice.

Q.

Why can't we have sweets for school?

A. Most schools don't allow children to have sweets. Sugar affects children in different ways. Some are fine and act as normal when they have eaten a truck load of sweets, but other children react differently. They become hyper, over excited, don't sit down or listen, and end up getting into trouble and being disruptive to everyone else. Also, most schools have a healthy eating policy and want to make sure that you are kept fit and healthy and go on to have a happy, healthy life! You can't blame your parents for not letting you take sweets to school; it's the school's fault, and your parents don't want you or themselves getting into trouble because you broke the rules!

A little of what you fancy does you good, so look forward to the sweet treats at the weekends or on special occasions. You'll have deserved them, and you'll have lovely healthy teeth!

Q. Why won't my parents let me get another pet? We only have two dogs and two cats, and I'd love a micro pig.

A. Micro pigs are very popular, cute, and tiny at the moment. Let's look at the set up you have at the moment. You have four pets that need a lot of looking after. How involved are you in looking after them, do you walk them, feed them, bring them to the vet's? I'm not sure what is involved in looking after a micro pig, but I'm sure it's just as much as having a new puppy. Perhaps your parents can't afford to look after another animal, they have enough to be feeding. Maybe they know that they will end up having to look after the pig when the novelty has worn off even if you promise that you will do it all the time.

Perhaps you need to wait until one of the pets you have already has gone off to pet heaven. So, for now enjoy the pets you have, look after them, love them, and help out with them as much as you possibly can.

If it's a pet that you might have in the future, do your homework. Check out what is involved in looking after a micro pig and be prepared to help and care for it as much as possible.

Q.

I'm thirteen years old, and I'm wondering why my parents are always on at me? If they didn't want to have to take care of me, they shouldn't have had me.

A.

Your parents had no idea how you were going to turn out when they were looking down at their beautiful newborn baby!! If they are having to get on at you to tidy up after yourself or do more around the house, then that is because you are lazy and not because they have stopped being your slaves. Your parents' job is to get you ready for the real world when you are living on your own and all of these responsibilities will be yours to take care of.

Parents, if you have a thirteen-year old who is not doing the jobs they should be, and you find yourself doing things that they could easily do themselves, make sure they do it. Stop babying them and give them the responsibility. There may be arguments, and it might take a while, but you and they will be better off for it in the end. These are life skills that your children need to have, and they need to help out in the house too.

So, parents, think of one thing that you know you are doing for your teenage child that they could easily do themselves and stick to it. It might take a couple of weeks to be become the normal routine, but it will happen and then you can move onto the next thing on the list that they can do themselves.

Thirteen-year-old son/daughter, do what you are expected to do and help out, your parents are not your slaves and will not always be there to do these things for you. You need to feel that you are growing up and taking responsibility for yourself. It will build your confidence and resilience for when you move out into the real world. Also, don't forget your parents have the ability to stop you from doing things you would like, or withholding money from you if need be, if you are not pulling your weight at home too.

No one wants to live in a house where there are arguments over little things, so help out, give everyone a break, and be happy.

Q. I'm eight years old, and I'm a bit worried that I won't get any presents. I've gotten into trouble a few times in school this year, and I do fight with my brother a lot. How can I make sure Santa doesn't forget me this year?!

A. To be honest, you need to make sure that you don't get into trouble and take responsibility for your own actions, then Santa will see that you are trying really hard and you won't be disappointed on Christmas morning. It's really tough, but try and walk away from arguments with your brother, and think about your behaviour in school.

Maybe you could try and do some extra help around the house for your parents. Keep your room clean, do a bit of tidying up, and keep out of fights with your brother and trouble in school.

You've got three weeks—loads of time to turn this around—and I'm sure Santa will see that you are really trying and you will be very happy and grateful on Christmas morning.

Q. Why are parents so strict?

A. There is a part of me that thinks parents grew up with strict parents and then they become parents and decide to do the same. If your parents are really strict, let them know! There are parents who decide that they are going to be really fun, never give out, and be like your best friend, but this doesn't really work either.

The main reason parents are so strict is because you, the children, keep doing stupid things! To stop you from doing things, we need to step in before you do it, or make sure you don't do it again. So, kids, stop doing stupid things, and they won't need to be so strict!

Q. I live in an apartment and don't have a chimney. Is this a problem for Santa?

A. No, it's not a problem at all. Santa has all sorts of magic tricks to get your presents to you. Personally, I think he has a special key that fits all locks and if he needs to use the front door he can, so he can get all the gifts to all the boys and girls and have a super Christmas. Hope he brings everything you hope for.

Q. I've asked Santa to not bring me any presents cause I want him to give them to homeless children. I'm a bit worried he'll still bring me something and I'll feel guilty if he does. What should I do if he brings me something?

A. It's lovely that you are thinking about other people who are in need and won't get anything for Christmas. Usually this is a time when children are only thinking about themselves and never give a thought to those who have nothing. If Santa brings you gifts on Christmas day, don't feel guilty as he is aware of how you feel about others, and maybe he'll make doubly sure that children who don't have a home will get something.

In the meantime, you could organise in your class a toy collection and donate them to a local shelter for families. If there are toys you get for Christmas or other gifts that perhaps your family won't use, donate these to a local charity. You should be very proud of yourself for being so selfless. Hope you have a wonderful Christmas.

Q. Kid question: school, what is the point?

A. This is a tough one to answer. Let's start with the official reply: you must go to school to learn, get an education, open your world to so much information, make friends, have fun, and maybe even go on to college and have a career.

You might get a teacher who may change your world and make school a really interesting place for you. It can also be tough at times, homework, exams. It can be hard for some children to be expected to sit all day and take in so much information. For some children, it is impossible to sit still for hours, and this can make school very hard and boring. Hopefully, more and more schools will start to change the way in which they teach a class, and it will become more inclusive for different types of learning.

Try and have fun, but don't be disruptive to other students trying to learn. You might surprise yourself and really love it in the end!

Q. Why does my dad smell worse than my mum?

A. Here's the dad sitting here and letting all mums and dads know that we do not smell worse, it's actually the mums who smell worse. You need to look long and hard at both of your parents as it's possible that your mum is blaming your dad for her smell too. It's not always about the dads being smelly, but the smelliest of all are the children!

Q. I am ten years old and have two little brothers. Why do I have to do everything around the house and they just get to play all the time? It's not fair!

A. I have a little brother, and growing up, I had to do most of the work and take more of the responsibility on while he got to play and have more fun! Unfortunately, this is part of being the eldest in a family, but it makes you become a very strong, resilient person for the future. And events that happen in the future may be easier for you to deal with than for your brothers as you have been building up experiences over the years because you are the eldest.

If it's really bothering you, then it's time to sit down with your parents and have a family meeting. Let them know how you feel, that you think they should be starting to do some small jobs around the house as you feel that it's all your responsibility, and you'd like some time to play too. See what happens. Hopefully, your parents will see what is going on, and your brothers will get some jobs to do too.

Q. How do I deal with a dad who is more bothered about himself than showing an interest in how me or my brother are? I tell him stuff, but he changes the subject and never fully listens.

A. This question came to me yesterday, only a couple of days after having a similar conversation with some colleagues about parents and how what they say to us can trigger feelings of frustration as if you were still a small child. What happens is when a parent says something to us as grown adults, we revert back to a childlike state and respond in that state instead of being an adult and ignoring the comment or just moving on. We still feel that our parents should always look after us and treat us in a certain manner, but this isn't always the case, and some parents are unable to do this.

If you are struggling with this, and it is a very deep issue and doesn't seem to be improving, then you may need to find some professional help. You are a young adult, you have control over this issue, and the tools to help you through it, so that you can continue to have a relationship with your dad and learn to deal with how he treats you and your brother in a manner that won't cause you any further hurt. Your happiness is very important and when someone close to you behaves in a manner that disrupts this, then you need to look after and protect your feelings. If your dad isn't a fatherly figure for you, and this is always the way it has been, then this can be really difficult, but now that you are an adult, not in their company all the time, it's alright for you to be disappointed in the way he behaves towards you.

It's ok to feel that your dad has let you down when it comes to needing a parent in your life who would be there for you to support, help, respect, and care for you. You need to stop expecting your dad to change and stop chasing a reality that isn't there for you and your dad. It's totally ok to not like your dad and to feel disappointment in him as a parent. You can always have a relationship with him, and it's in your control as to how that relationship continues. It's doesn't need to be deep or emotional, you can keep it at an emotional state that works best for you. If you are struggling with the emotional side of this new relationship with your dad, then it may be good to chat to someone about it, talk to someone impartial about it who has no experience with you or your life. You will need to build a different relationship with your dad that works for you, and you will be ok emotionally and have a better long-term relationship with your dad.

It's not your job to change your dad regardless of how long his behaviour has been like this or how hard it is to be around him. You don't need to put up with him, and it's ok to keep a bit of distance. Be there when it's really necessary, but for now, look after yourself and you will have a better relationship with your dad.

Q. I'm fifteen and my parents fight constantly. I'm about to start my junior certificate. I tried to talk to both of them separately about having the house calm when they've asked if there's anything they can do to help me study, but it just doesn't seem to make any difference. I'm talking to them less and less, as both of them always turn whatever I bring up to something about them and how hard things are for them. I'm at the stage now where I kinda wish they would split up just so the arguing will stop. I try not to cause any hassle in the house cause it's just not worth it, but my friends are telling me to just go crazy at them and that might make them see me and not just themselves. I'm so confused and it's really distracted me from my study. Have you any advice?

A. It's clear that your parents are so caught up in their own issues that they have lost sight of you and the impact that their behaviour is having on you. This happens when partners fight, and it's not about you, so although their behaviour may seem very selfish, it's not as a result of anything you have done. It's time to sit down with your parents and explain to them how their behaviour is affecting you, your life and your study for the exams coming up. It's difficult to know what your parents are fighting about, it could be money issues, bad patch, or perhaps like you say, maybe they do need some time apart to see where their relationship is going. It's seems as if you are trying to keep your head down and not cause any problems and as a result of this your parents probably don't have to keep you in mind as they continue to fight over their own issues.

I suggest you write a letter to both of them and outline how all of this is affecting you—not blaming them for anything or being nasty towards them—but just putting down exactly how their behaviour is causing you worry, hurt, and sadness. Let them know that you are under pressure with your exams and the studying, and that their fighting is only making the situation a lot harder for you.

Your friends may be advising you to go crazy at them, but it seems as if that's not the type of person you are, and that doing this could make the situation a lot worse. Give the letters to them separately and let them digest it.

If you are struggling to study in the house while your parents are fighting, could you possibly go somewhere else to study? Is there a friend, family member, or library close by where you could go to study?

You can't control the fighting, or if they possibly break up, but what you can do by writing a letter is put it in black and white for them to see how hurt you are. Reading the letter means they have to stop, sit down and concentrate on what they are reading, and as a result, they should be able to see how this is affecting you emotionally. They may not have been aware of how upset you are, but when it is in your handwriting and in front of their eyes, it becomes very real.

See what happens. You shouldn't have to worry about any of this, especially when you already have so much on your plate. Hopefully this will work, and you will be able to sit down and talk to your parents. You will all need to be open with each other, and don't forget you have done nothing wrong, and as parents, they should be behaving better.

MANAGING
BEHAVIOUR

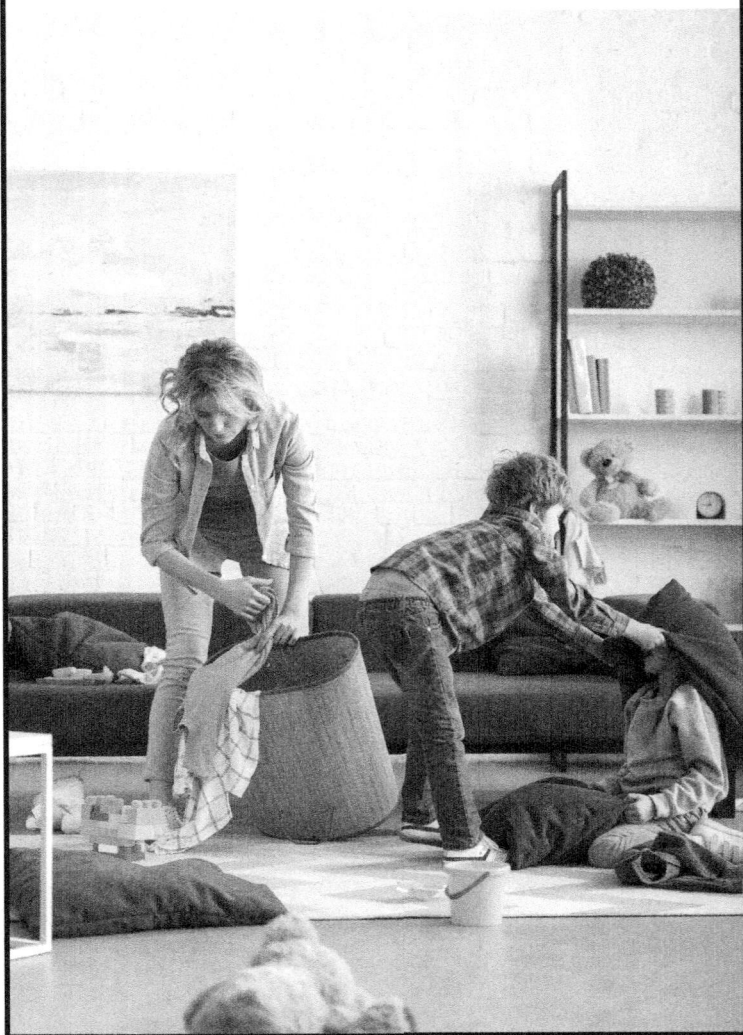

Q. My son, who is ten, and daughter, who is eight, generally get on quite well, but we've been finding that recently our daughter has been trying to "get her brother in trouble" by coming and telling us little tales that we either know about or are not important for us to have to deal with. We know what she is doing and have tried speaking to her about it and let her know that that is not okay. Have you any suggestions on how to deal with it so we can nip it in the bud? Our son for the most part doesn't seem that bothered, but when he's a bit stressed or tired you can see that it gets to him.

A. It's important that we nip these behaviours in the bud while they are still small issues and not developing into something more serious. It's normal behaviour for a younger child to try and get an older sibling into trouble because from an early age they know they are younger, more vulnerable, and can get away with more! As the parent, you need to pull your daughter up on this behaviour and that it's not ok to do this to their brother. It's not ok to get someone else in trouble for no reason. It's not ok for your daughter to get contentment from seeing her brother get into trouble especially if he hasn't done anything to deserve a punishment.

Let's set boundaries. Your daughter is old enough to understand consequences for her behaviour and that they will be put in place if she comes to you with every little tittle tattle on her brother. If it's something really big, like he hit her or called her something really nasty, then she can let you know and you will deal with it. Small things like not tidying away a cup or leaving a bit of rubbish down somewhere are not things to tell on, but more serious things are. Let your daughter know that you acknowledge what she has said to you and that you will deal with it. It is not up to her to decide the punishment or take into her own hands.

You may need to look at the way you treat both your children when it comes to punishments. It's very easy, without us noticing, to favour a younger child. The younger child will know this and use it to the best of their advantage, which can leave an older child feeling vulnerable and not protected. Perhaps sit them both down and let them know that you parent them equally, there are no favourites, and bad behaviour towards each other is not acceptable. Let them know that sometimes you get it right, and sometimes you get it wrong, but it's up to you to apologise for this and be the parent.

You need to let your daughter know that if she continues to treat her brother in this way she will be the child being punished even though she feels her brother is in the wrong. It may take a little bit of work, but it will help all relationships for the future, and build respect between your son and daughter.

Q. School nights we generally have the kids turn off screens around 7:30-7:45. Mary C goes to bed around 8:30 and the boys between 9:15-9:30pm. This may seem early, but remember they are up before 6:00am.

Anyway, Thursday evening screens went off at 7:30. MC got ready for bed, and she generally reads for about 15-20 minutes before lights out. That night she came down to the kitchen just after 8pm and said she was ready to go to sleep because she wanted to be well-rested for school the next day. Now, before you think I'm completely naive, there were some special activities scheduled the next day as part of Catholic Schools Week. I was also in the middle of cleaning up the kitchen, so my mom radar was not operating at full capacity. I said, "Ok, I'll be up in a minute to tuck you in." Her dad and I did, and came back downstairs.

I noticed her hair ribbons on the kitchen counter, so took them up to her room. As I'm walking in/out of her room I hear some sort of talking.

I pause and ask, "What is that?"
She replies, "Rory must be watching a video."

"No, I think the sound is in this room." So, I walk over toward her bed and see a faint glow under the covers.

I pull back the covers and find her tablet. "Mary Christen Elizabeth," I exclaim (yes, it was a full name offense) and confiscate the illegal goods. "We will discuss this tomorrow. Good night."

I did not yell. I was honestly too taken off-guard that my angel had deceived me, AND tried to throw her brother under the bus.

I think I've been more upset by the fact my youngest, my baby, had deliberately lied and had been sneaky than over what she actually did. We've had this issue multiple times with the boys trying to use electronics when they shouldn't that I'm honestly a bit immune to the crime.

I really do feel like I've lost some last piece of my kids' innocence or something. I can't really put it in words, other than it makes me a bit sad. Kind of like when your youngest starts school or something. There was a calm discussion and consequences, but that innocence can't be regained.

A. It sounds as if this event has really impacted you, and what it highlighted for me, is that firstly, when it came to managing the situation you kept yourself together. No shouting and disruption of the bedtime routine for the whole family, and a calm message to your child that you will discuss it in the morning. You handled it really well in the moment. Secondly, the other part that really stood out for me was the realization for you that you are losing a part of your child's innocence, and that your daughter is growing up. We don't always, as parents, notice these small changes in our children that mark a turning point in their development into older children and ultimately young adults. This can have a big impact on some parents, and if they don't accept it, and realise that they will be dealing with an older child with different issues, they may lose focus and not see how their parenting needs to evolve for this next step of their child's development.

I have been back and forth with this parent to discuss the situation, and although this may be off topic a bit in relation to the situation, I feel it's very important to highlight the importance of parents dealing with their children growing up and accepting it.

Some parents can become too emotionally upset by the fact that their child is growing up. They were happy with them being a certain age, and for their world not to change, but it's a part of growing up for everyone, and you need to learn to let it go, be happy your child is developing, and not dwell too much on what is now behind you. As a parent you will need to grow with your child and develop new parenting skills to help you with this new stage of your child's life. You need to be able to help them, keep them safe, and make sure the boundaries are in place, because as they get older, they will learn to test them more and more, which is natural, but they will need to know that you are still there to stop them and pull them back in if they go too far.

It's ok to feel the emotions of your child not being a small child anymore, but you need to be mature in your thoughts and actions towards your child and be happy they are moving on. They will always want you and need you, it may not be as frequent as before, but it's why you have children to watch them grow and equip them to be ready for the world and have their own life.

Q. Yes, Wicked Witch made a return yesterday evening. To be fair, she was provoked by teens and a long day driving through pouring rain.

It started in the morning over breakfast. My middle child's usual method of irritating me is to just chip away at something. He doesn't yell or really loose his temper, just continues to complain and/or argue until I get fed up. Now, I handle this far better than I used to, but before 6am I am not at my most patient. Yesterday morning's complaint was how we never go anywhere for Spring Break and every other kid in his class goes to the beach or somewhere. It continued in a back/forth fashion that resulted in Sean actually saying if he was that unsatisfied, then he could find somewhere else to live. And I chimed in about how I'm tired of no one appreciating what they have. No, my husband shouldn't have yelled, and I shouldn't have even engaged in a pointless argument with an almost fourteen-year old.

Act 2: I'm driving my sixteen-year old to school, and asked him about an assignment. He doesn't respond because he's too busy watching something on his phone. I ask again and the discussion turns to how he should be working to be more involved in activities around what he's interested in doing in Film/TV production. He turns down every suggestion I have because it isn't exactly what he hopes to do. I say, "no it's not, but it's experience and you need to work toward building a resume." To which he replies quite sarcastically and disrespectfully, "No crap!" I, of course, respond with the usual parenting line of, "Don't speak to me that way," and "I hope you don't talk that way to other adults," and followed up with, "You need to be putting forth some effort, hard work pays off." We arrive at school and he slams out of the car without a word. I call out "Have a good day," and now I'm irritated with 2/3 of my ungrateful children within a one hour period.

Act 3: I arrive home just before 4pm after driving to/from a town about two hours away for a work meeting. It's been pouring rain all day, and I'm just tired. I head up to my office to return a couple of emails and find my eldest in the sitting/ TV area playing Xbox. His room is the usual disaster, and he is currently failing three classes, so I'm sure there are assignments he should be working on. I tell him to get off the console. My daughter is playing on the computer, and I ask if her homework is done (it is). Then I remind her what the house rules are about electronics—she stomps off to her room. She comes into my office a minute later to report it's not fair, my middle son is on his iPad in his room. Well, at this point I head on over to the negative triangle.

I call the three of them over to the sitting area. I remind them of our house rules regarding electronics (not related to schoolwork) on school nights, and I tell them there is now a new rule: no console at all Monday–Thursday. All three have spent way too much time on it lately due to weather, school holidays, and my illness, allowing things to slip. I point out that as grades are slipping all around, we need to refocus.

So, here's where I'm at (driving provided some thinking time):

1. I don't really regret the conversation about electronics that has needed saying for about two weeks. I could have come at it from a more positive angle, but some straight talk was needed. I will strive to approach in a more positive triangle manner as we move forward.

2. My teenagers need some real world exposure. Forcing them to work in a homeless shelter will probably result in resentment and not provide the lesson we're hoping for. I want to have a discussion with both boys about looking ahead to summer plans. There are ample opportunities for both to gain work experience through both volunteering and paying positions. I would like to give them a chance to put together their own plan for what they would like to do over the summer, and then my husband and I can help them put it into action.

3. We have spent so much time trying to get our eldest on track academically, which doesn't seem to really be working, that we've neglected to encourage him to get involved with other activities. My middle child needs to come to terms with the fact he is not going to to the school he wants to go to. We need to arrange an appointment to get him properly registered, so we will coordinate having someone speak to

him about different activities, clubs, so he can start exploring his passions.

Tired of reading yet???

Yes, I have been reminding myself that there is no such thing as a perfect parent, AND we make the best decisions at the time with the information we have. It really was just a perfect storm of a day.

A. I really felt for this parent, and I'm sure a lot of you can relate to her problem. Sometimes it feels as if there is no break, things just keep building up and building up and then a perfect storm of rubbish events happen and everything explodes.

You feel as if you want to pack a bag, walk out the door, and never look back. Of course, in reality, this never happens.

I did get in touch with this parent separately, and as we were chatting through the events, it became clear that she had managed to deal with the situation very well. She sat all the children down and reminded them about the boundaries and how they work in the household. This is a reminder that children have short memories at this age and don't always remember about consequences, especially as they are only really concerned about what it going on in their lives, and don't see how their behavior can have a bigger impact on the whole family. You need to revisit the consequences with your children just to let them know that they are still in place and need to be respected.

It was really positive that this parent stepped in and reminded the children of the boundaries and introduced a new one because things had slipped. So, this parent then had to take responsibility and bring the line back, so the children were made aware that the parents are serious about the behavior of the children, and it was not going to be tolerated. This is good and will probably not need to be in place for too long as the children will get the message that you are serious about consequences and about changing the behavior in the household for the good of everyone.

It's ok to have these days, no one is perfect, and setbacks will happen. It's good for this parent to take stock, have a look at what's going on, and try to remedy it. When we are under stress we can easily get into a tug of war battle with our children and it can be draining. To be able to step out of it and get control as the parent and let your children know that you won't tolerate the behavior is great but not always easy!

As parents, this couple is trying to do the best for their child as they see fit at the present time. If it doesn't work out and changes need to be made, then it can be looked at again, but you as the parents have the final say. You've set the reset button with your children, so for now you feel as if you have been clear about the boundaries and they are clear about it, too, so hopefully this will be a positive result for everyone.

Q. My six-year old is a great, fun, little boy. He's always up for a laugh, but recently he's been burping out loud a lot. At first it was funny, but we have a big family event coming up soon, and his grandparents would really frown upon him burping in public like that. How do I get him to stop?! Everyone laughs when he does it, so he can't see why it's wrong sometimes to burp.

A. That's the big thing, when children do funny things like burping, farting, or swearing for the first time, people will always laugh and it's contagious! At some point you do need to stop this behavior and learn when it's an appropriate time to do it and when it's not, like out in public at a dinner, or in school when a teacher is trying to teach. It's clear for this parent that this needs to stop, especially when it's really necessary, and usually with most children of this age, this is a phase and they will grow out of it.

You can have a conversation with him and let him know that what's he is doing is funny and when you are all at home and having fun, it makes everyone laugh, but there are times when it's not ok, and there are people who won't find it funny and may give out to you if you keep doing it. Explain that some people find it rude and not the thing to do if you are out to dinner or in class. Let your son know that it's not something you want to have to give him a consequence for, like taking away a device or limiting tv time, so if he can learn to keep the burps at home and not in school or in public, that would be great. Test him out, go out in public and see did he listen and not burp when you were out and about. If he does that's fantastic, but if he doesn't, well, you may need to look at a consequence, something that meets the behavior. He's only six, will grow out of it, and if you stop laughing at him when he does it, he will soon see that everyone is bored of him and he'll move on, hopefully not to something worse!

Q. I don't have any kids myself, but my sister has three youngsters aged between three and eight. They're great kids. The older two are boys and are typical lads, and the youngest is a girl, and she just wants to be like the boys. From where I'm looking, my sister doesn't seem to be able to handle them, and she loses it and shouts quite a bit at them. I've asked her if I can help her, but she just says no and that everything is fine. I'm worried that my sister isn't handling things well and that the kids are learning that shouting and screaming is the normal way to handle situations. There doesn't seem to be much in the way of boundaries in the house. Have you any suggestions on how I can help my sister out?

A. One of the most difficult things with any children that are not your own is watching from the outside looking in and seeing that maybe things aren't quite right in the family. Sometimes you may have unanswered questions in terms of whether or not a certain style of parenting is right or could be done differently. The fact that you are aware that things are not quite right for your sister and her children shows that perhaps there is something going on that needs a bit of attention. Having children can be really stressful at times and we can have awful days as parents when it feels as if we've done nothing but scream and shout all day and got nowhere fast!

There will be parents listening to this and their advice would be that you should stay out of it, you don't have children so you can't fully understand what your sister is going through.

It's very difficult to sit back and watch what's going on especially as you love your sister and her children so much and want them to be ok. What you've witnessed may just be one of those periods when things are really stressful, lots going on, and no break in sight. Does your sister have other supports? You don't mention whether or not her husband/partner is around.

There are subtle ways of helping out your sister without making her feel she's getting help. You could offer to take the children for a night or two every now and again, or for a day at the weekend that would allow your sister to have a break, time away from them and the home. You could have a chat with her and see if there are any evening courses she would like to do, or maybe exercise classes, yoga, and you could offer to take the children on these evenings if there is no partner/husband available.

When the children are with you, it's your rules in your home or for the time you are minding them. Let them know that they have to behave in a certain way and then this becomes normal for them. If this works, then it's possible it may feed into how they behave in their own home. If your sister asks how you got on, tell her that they had to do as she asked and it worked out well, but make sure you don't tell her that you can parent them better then her!

Keep in touch with your sister, keep asking if she needs help, and take the kids off her hands every now and again, even if it's only to go for a walk and grab an ice cream. Maybe even just take your sister out, go for a meal, have a chat, but not necessarily about the kids. Your sister may just be in a fog of looking after the children and doesn't even realise she needs a break or some help, so little bits of help that she doesn't even notice might just be what she needs to get her through this really busy time.

Q. I and my family love the summer. We love getting out and about and having tons of fun. The only thing about the summer that drives me nuts is the return of the ice cream vans. Twice a day, every day, they are around our estate and my heart is broken with my kids tormenting me for ice cream, and it does seem like every other child in the estate is getting ice cream off the van twice a day. How do I stop my kids from pestering me every day?

A. Summer and the ice cream van...even when I hear them I want one as we didn't have the money to get one when we were growing up.

If you are ok with your child having an ice cream once or twice a week during the summer, then make a summer ice cream pact with them and let them know that twice a week they can have one from the vans, but if they pester you outside of the ice cream days, then you take a day away or two if they keep it up. The horror of seeing a sibling enjoying their lovely ice cream will be enough for them to stop pestering you, and if they don't, well, there won't be ice cream all summer and they will have to live with that decision. You need to stick to your decision and hopefully this will lead to lovely excitement when the ice cream van comes around. Your children will learn lessons such as having to wait for something and boundaries in terms of how they need to behave in order to be rewarded. Enjoy the ice cream!

Q. I have a six-year-old who just refuses to brush her teeth. I've tried punishing her and bribing her but nothing seems to work. I don't have the time in the morning to be standing over her. Tell me there's a simple solution to this please!

A. The biggest thing here to remember is that it's going to take a bit of work and time to get this part of your child's daily routine. You might need to look at a combination of a few things. Firstly, if she's not doing it and you don't have the time to stand over her, you may need to look at getting up ten minutes earlier for the next little while so you can make time in your morning schedule to be with her while she brushes her teeth. Keep reminding her that you shouldn't have to stand over and watch her do her teeth as she is old enough to do it herself. At first she may love having you with her while she does it, but this will wear off. Most habits and changes in a routine take about fourteen days to be permanent, so try this for a couple of weeks. Get used to having to smell her breath, check that she's done it, and then if she does, have a run of doing it without asking. Reward her, not sweets, but something that she really enjoys.

Try and get the morning going well and then transfer this into the evening, too, which can be harder when they are tired and just want to go to bed.

If your child is not doing something although they are old enough to do it, then it's up to you as a parent to step in and make a routine of being there, so they do it, reward when it's been accomplished, and help them keep up the good work!

SAFETY
(ONLINE & OFFLINE)

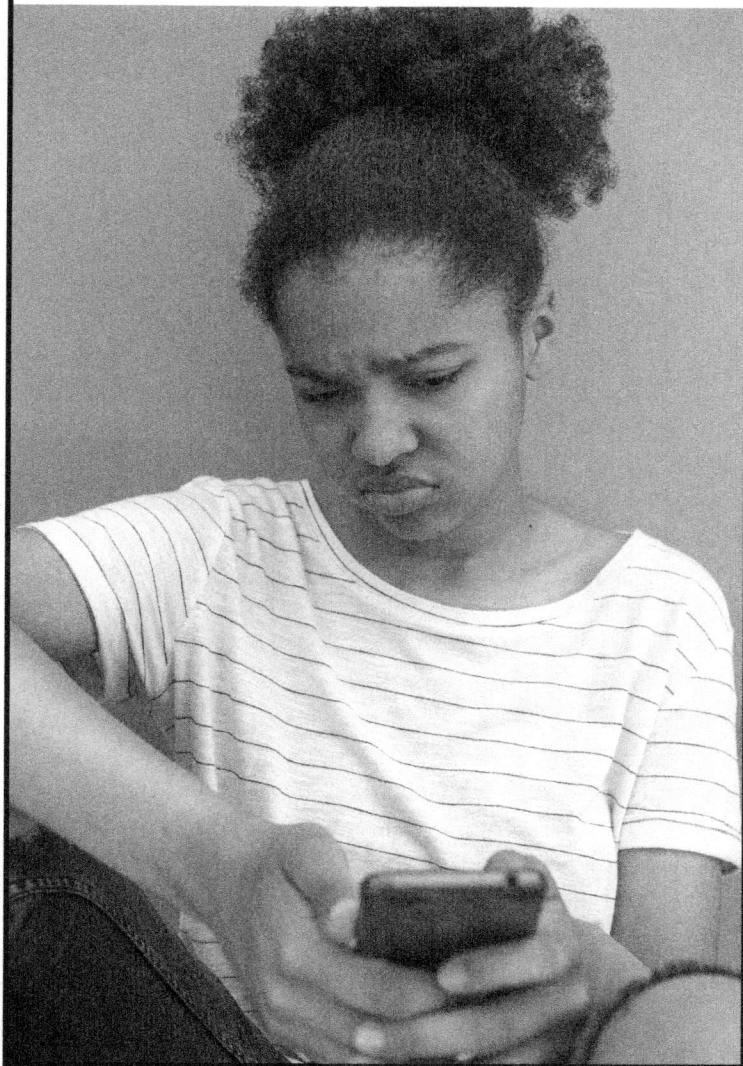

Q.

My son is getting his first mobile phone for Christmas, and both me and my husband are nervous about him getting it. What advice can you give us around how to manage this as best we can?

A.

Getting a phone is such a big deal now for children and parents. It's a big step into a new world, contact with other people, and a lot of unknown areas too. There are so many scary stories out there that make it a worrying time for parents, especially as their children will be online without their guidance or knowledge.

First things first, you have a bit of time to do your homework in terms of safeguarding your child while they are using their phone. You can start to have conversations with your child about the boundaries that will be put in place with regard to use of the phone. Talk through the rules, these will be there to keep your child safe and not to put a damper on them getting a phone. Talk about the apps they may like to have on their phone. I'm not sure how old your child is, but a number of apps have age restrictions, and if you are not happy with your child getting a particular app, then you can let them know that you won't be downloading it on their phone and that they won't be able to do it themselves.

If your child has a list of apps, you can look into them, see if they are appropriate for your child, especially in terms of their age. We can give in to our kids so easily and we don't want them to feel that they are being left out, but if you give your child unlimited access to social media with no restrictions, they are going to see content that is not suitable, that their brains will not be able to process. So, if you are going to let your child use social media, what are they allowed to access, is it suitable, and what are the boundaries you are going to put in place to keep their social media usage safe?

There are a number of apps that you can download to monitor your child's use of social media. It can look for words, images that your child may have received in texts and messages, and see if they are inappropriate and need to be highlighted. This not only lets you keep them safe from others, but it's a great way to see how your child is conducting themselves on social media too. Your child will need to be aware that once something is sent out there, it's out there, and even if you delete the message from your phone, it's still available on the internet.

If you are allowing your child access to the internet, you may want to restrict what they can look at. We all want our children to be aware of the world around us, but they can also be a couple of clicks away from viewing material such as porn or murder that's not appropriate and may cause anxiety in your child. It is very simple to restrict the content your child is allowed to search online and they may need to ask your permission to allow them to view a certain site. It may seem crazy to have to monitor their searches, but the internet is a very interesting place, it is both good and bad, and as a parent, you want your child to get all the positives out of it until they are old enough and mature enough to know that the downside of the internet is something they are not interested in.

Now you have the time, do your research, and be happy with your decision about the phone for your child. If you put the work in now, have the conversations with your child about the phone and the boundaries, you are less likely to have arguments in the future. Having a phone is a big step on the ladder of growing up and you need to trust that your child will be responsible. Have the conversation about how they conduct themselves online, in texts and messages, and also to be careful about the information they give out to others—especially personal information. They may think they are just having a one-on-one conversation with a friend, when in actual fact, the whole world can have access to your messages. Any information they put online is there forever, so they need to think twice before they post something. Also if they can see online bullying going on in a chat they are in, make sure they don't get involved. Let them know that you are there for them to discuss what they may have read and how they feel about it. If it's something serious, a parent may need to get involved.

Keep chatting to your child about the phone, what they are doing, and keep reminding them about the boundaries. Try not to let them on it all the time, have phone breaks, and not to have the phone in the bedroom at night even if they are only using it as an alarm!

Q. My ten-year-old son has recently got Snapchat and I'm a bit concerned about what he will be sending to others and what he will be sent. We let him have it as all his friends have it and he was feeling left out. Any advice on how to manage this?

A. This will resonate with a lot of parents who have children that want particular social media apps as all their friends have them and they are being teased because they don't. There are a lot of positives to social media, but there are downsides too. As parents, we don't want our children to be upset, for them to be left out or bullied because they are doing something different. We need to think if our children are emotionally developed enough to be able to handle the content they may see or receive on an app like Snapchat.

When we were younger, we didn't have any social media or even the internet to deal with. If there was someone in our school annoying us or bullying us, we went home and didn't have to deal with them again until the next day. But with phones and social media, this bullying can potentially be with your child every minute of the day with no switch off, especially if they aren't telling you over fear of losing a phone.

You need to take responsibility for your child and their social media use. If you feel they are not ready yet to deal with the possible content they will receive, or cannot be mature enough in their own relationships online, then it's not the time for your child to have an app like Snapchat. I get a number of children referred to me for anxiety, and a number of these cases are because of social media use—not just bullying online, but also not being able to process the more adult content they are seeing. Subjects that you have probably never had a conversation about with your child such as sex, porn, and murder will all of a sudden be more available for your child to view, and if you haven't discussed what is appropriate and isn't appropriate for your child to see, then their heads will become overloaded and confused as they try to figure out if this is right or wrong.

Sending your child online without proper supervision or conversations about what they are doing online will lead to problems further down the line, and if you chose to ignore your child's online life at an early age, you will more than likely be dealing with issues over anxiety, bullying.

Your child may get teased in school for not having social media and may be angry with you, but if you feel they and you are not ready to be in that world yet, then that is your right as their parent, and it's just a part of life.

Take the time to research the apps your child is looking to have. Is there an age limit for signing up? Are there more age appropriate apps to start with? Do you have a monitoring app connected to your child's device so you can get alerts if they receive something you feel may be harmful or content that they may be sending out too?

Do your research, it's important as their parent to keep them safe. Teaching them how to use social media properly is just as important as teaching them to cross the road safely. If you notice a change in their behaviour as they use more social media, you will have to talk to them about it, perhaps limit their time on their device.

Q. My daughter who's eleven, keeps talking to me about wanting to be an Instagram or YouTube influencer. I've no idea what she is talking about. I want to keep her safe and don't want her sharing everything about her life, but at the same time I don't want to block her dream. What should I do?

A. Firstly, you need to educate yourself on what it is your child would like to do. Do a bit of homework and have a look on YouTube and Instagram at the people your child would like to be like. It is suitable, is it something you think she is too young for? What are the comments like from people who follow the influencers, could your child deal with the responses?

Have a chat with your daughter and find out what she would like her content to be on YouTube and Instagram.

Talk about the information that can't be online such as family details, phone numbers, addresses, date of birth. Have a serious discussion about the photos she puts online and that they are appropriate.

If you feel that after having these discussions you are happy for her to have a YouTube or Instagram account, start small and only allow access to family or very close friends for a bit until she gets used to it, and then review it and see if you can allow her to have wider audience access.

Her behaviour and how she conducts herself online will have an influence on how you feel it should progress. If you feel she has become too involved in it, then perhaps you will need to introduce time limits and only at weekends.

Keep an eye on her, chat to her regularly about what she is doing online, and check the accounts every now and again. She is a child, she needs supervision, and that's up to you as her parent.

SEPARATION & DIVORCE

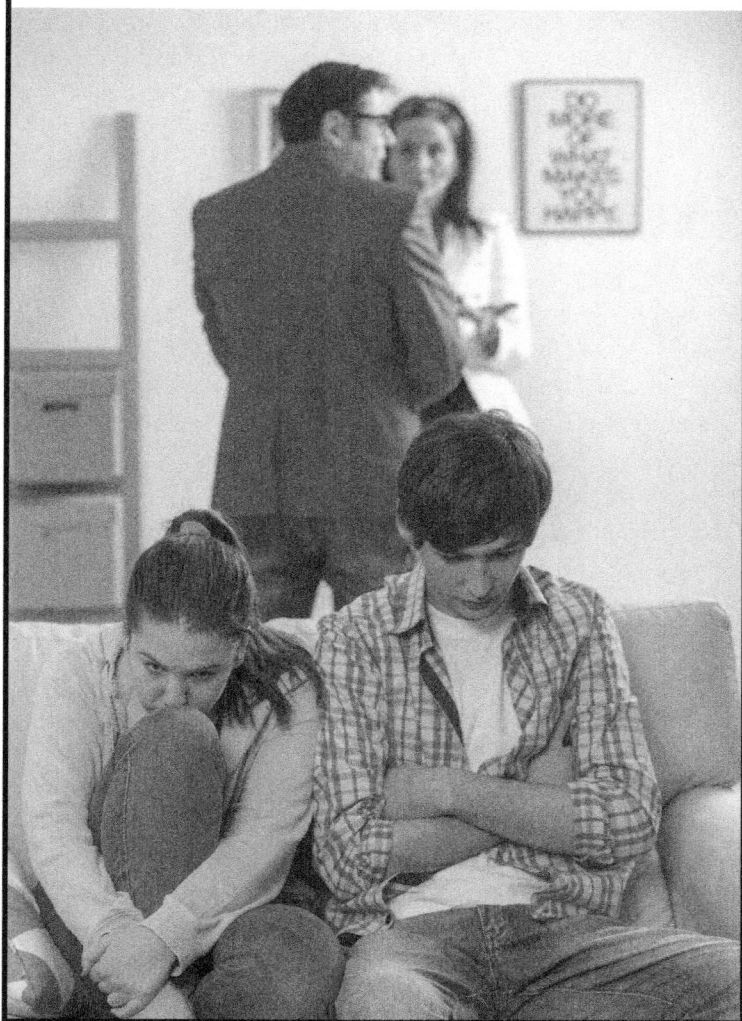

Q. I'm at my wit's end. Myself and my husband separated last October and it's been a messy break up. I've tried to be level-headed and fair, but he keeps pushing and trying to undermine me. Financially, I've been left with very little, so don't have as much disposable income as my ex, and he tries to buy our son "things." I got my son a big Easter egg, but he arrived home from his Dad's this evening proclaiming that Dad had got him a brand new console for Easter. I couldn't believe it. I feel so down about this. Is there anything I can do?

A. This is a really difficult, frustrating situation to be in, especially as you are not only dealing with the break up, but also the change in your financial situation, and now trying to live by your means that you have available to you.

Firstly, you may need to get some emotional support for yourself in order to be able to deal with the break up. You have stated that you are financially struggling, but there are counsellors who will provide reduced-rate services—you may just need to be a bit of searching. This will benefit you greatly, and you need this support at the moment. This situation is bigger than just an Easter egg, and you may be tested again and again in the future and it's how you learn to deal with these situations that will make life either easier or harder for you. It sounds as if your ex is testing you and letting you know that he has a certain amount more power over you and your son because he has more money and can therefore provide more for your child. This is a cruel and childish way to behave and has nothing to do with the welfare of your child, he may just be trying to get at you.

You don't want your child to be put in a position where they have to pick a parent. It's not fair, and they should never have to choose. You could sit down with your child and chat about the gift and let them know how lucky they are to get it. Let them know that things have now changed in the household and that although you can't buy them big gifts, you can always be there for them. Help them whenever they need it, always have a kiss and a cuddle for them, or an ear to listen to any of

Separation & Divorce

their problems.

Your child is a child, and they may just want stuff and that's it. You will need to try and explain as best you can to them that money is tight and big gifts will be at Christmas or birthdays and that if there is something they would like they would save for it and buy it. If your child is struggling with the break up, they may need support too. Let the school know what is going on, they may have some resources.

Finally you may need to have a conversation with your ex. That doesn't mean you have to tell him what he can and can't buy for your child, that's not really possible. You can have a conversation about what your child's expectations are in terms of gifts. Perhaps let him know that before the break up, big expensive gifts were bought at Christmas and birthdays, and that you don't want your child getting spoilt. You are going to have to come to an agreement on how you are going to co-parent going forward as it is easier now to let your child know how things will be, but if you continue to spoil your child now, it will become so much more difficult in the future as they get older and want more and more.

1. Contact your ex and discuss the expectations levels you are setting for your child and the impact this may have on them, and then when you have done this, you need to let it go because you have no control over what he does.

2. Sit down with your child and talk about how the size or value of the gift does not show the amount of love that someone has for somebody.

3. Do you need emotional support to help you with the separation, to make you stronger, and help you get through this tough time?

Q. I have suspected increasing disharmony in my brother & sister-in-law's marriage for about a year—and unfortunately, these suspicions were confirmed over Easter weekend. I will not get into all the specifics of their discord, but they have some serious issues to resolve. The resulting conflict meant that only my brother and his children attended Easter dinner at my house even though my sister-in-law's parents were in attendance.

My question is this - my kids at seventeen, fourteen, and nearly ten, are old enough to realize that something is seriously wrong. We don't discuss it openly around them, but they have likely overheard some comments made by their parents and grandparents around the situation. This is my first experience with someone so close to me to have marriage difficulties on this level, so I'm at a bit of a loss. We definitely don't think our kids need all the details, but I think we should say something to them. Perhaps individually as their ages may warrant different levels of discussion? Any advice you have would be welcomed.

A. This can be a difficult situation to see unfold, especially as you are on the outskirts of it, but you can see more clearly that there are issues going on and they are close family members. As a parent, you wouldn't normally think of having to have a discussion with your own children about the problems in another family members home, but as you say they are older and more aware of how people behave around each other.

Do you feel it is appropriate to talk to your children about their aunt and uncle's relationship? What is it you feel they need to know? If they are still together as a couple and are just working through some tough issues, is there any reason why you need to discuss this with your children? What are you going to tell them? Are you going to say that they are having marriage difficulties, which then sort themselves out and you needn't have said anything? What impact will this news have on your children and how they then see their relationship with their aunt and uncle? Your older children may start to ask more questions as to why they are having problems, and these may be questions you can't answer as you are not privy to the personal lives of your relatives. Maybe it's ok just to say that they may just be going through a rough patch, working through some things, and really it's none of our business, so it's normal relationships all round for us unless you are told something different by them.

Your relatives shouldn't feel that they need to clarify or tell anyone what is going on in their lives unless they are looking for advice or help. The steps that follow need to be done on a need-to-know basis, and that's when you will know if you need to have further conversations with your children in relation to their aunt and uncle's marriage. You will then be there to answer any questions they have or concerns about their relatives' relationship.

Q. My children's mother has been stopping the children from seeing me. She keeps making excuses for them to miss my time with them, and it's breaking my heart. I've had to go to court to try and see my kids (even though my wife had an affair, and I had to leave my family home and kids!). I'm so frustrated with how slow the whole system is when all I want to do is see my children. How can I make her see sense and just let me see my kids? I accept that the relationship is over and have no interest in getting back with her, but she's still hurting me on a daily basis through my kids.

A. This is something that, unfortunately, has become increasingly regular amongst separating couples. There has been a marital breakup, and more often than not, the husband/dad leaves the family home and the wife/mum takes on the role of most of the child rearing. Sometimes if the relationship ended badly and there is a lot of resentment and anger towards one of the people, then, unfortunately, the children get used as a way of hurting the other person. Sadly, the best interests of the children has been lost, and how they are adjusting to this new family dynamic is not recognized as one parent is too busy trying to hurt the other parent over the separation. When your focus is just on hurting a person, you lose sight of the really important things such as making sure your children are ok, and this would include making sure they have time with the other parent, too, regardless of how much hurt you may feel towards them. This isn't just about your hurt and your relationship with an ex, it is also about moving forward and making sure that everyone gets to see both parents.

This, of course, is very difficult, and I can only imagine that this has been a very tough and upsetting experience for you and your children.

The system in Ireland in relation to divorce and children usually sides with the mum/wife, and there is a feeling that they are better off with their mum in these circumstances. This, of course, isn't always the case. Most children need to be around both of their parents especially if relationships have always been good and there is no reason for them not to be in contact.

It can be such a confusing time for children, especially if they are not aware of there being problems in the relationship, and all of a sudden their parents aren't living together and they are not getting to see their dad as often. This can have such a negative impact on them in the short term, and the long term. It is so important to put the children first initially, and make sure they are ok, getting to see both parents regularly and know that they will be ok.

It is an awful, hurtful way of getting back at someone by not letting them see their children. It doesn't solve anything for the children, yourself, or your ex, and should never happen.

You need to try and communicate this to your ex. You need to let her know that you need to see your children, and that it's very important for them and for you. Let her know that you need to put aside your problems for a bit and make sure the children are ok. If your ex is breaching her court order in terms of your access to the children, then you will need to let your solicitor know. It is a very slow, unfair system in Ireland in relation to separation and divorce. Have your children's best interests at heart, and keep this with you always. Let the judge know that you are trying to do everything you can to keep your children safe, loved, and cared for.

Perhaps write a journal every day noting how much you love your children, what they mean to you, and how much you look forward to spending time with them. Don't write down any negative words about your ex, just lovely thoughts about them and how you love them. Then give it to them, they may think you are bonkers, but if they read it, they will see that you are there for them and always thinking of them.

It's a very tough situation you are in and I hope it works out for you and your children.

Q. So I'm a grown woman and I don't really know why I'm emailing you, but I'm about to get married to my fiancé. We've been so looking forward to the big day, but inside I'm dreading it. The reason I feel this way is because my parents don't speak to each other. They've been divorced for ten years, but there is still so much bad blood between them that they literally cannot be in the same room together. Our big day is approaching and all I can think about is praying they don't even cross paths and ruin the day. This is really upsetting me, and I'm at a loss as to what to do.

A. I've worked with both sides on this issue. I've worked with the parents who won't talk to each other at special occasions, and I always pull them up on it and point out to them that the day isn't about them, it's about someone else and their happiness. We talk about how the parents, or just even one parent, can plan out the day so they are civil to each other and their child won't have to worry about their behavior and can have the lovely memories they are supposed to have on such an important day of their life.

Being the child of separated parents on your very special day, when they don't get along, can be extremely stressful and something that you should never have to be worrying about. Your focus shouldn't be on them and how they are going to behave.

It might be time to sit down with both your parents before the big day, go out for lunch, and have an honest and open conversation with them about the day and how much you are looking forward to sharing it with them. Let them know how happy you are that they will both be there, and then let them know that you are not going to put up with any of their fighting. Explain that you are well aware that they don't get on together and that the wedding would be one of those occasions when something could happen, but they have to put it aside for one day for you. If they feel that this won't be possible, then one or both of them need to decide not to come, because you would prefer for them not to be there if they are going to be off with each other and cause an atmosphere. Let them know that you shouldn't be stressed and worrying about them and how they are going to behave. They are not children! Let them know that your focus should be on all the great things that are going to happen, all the fun and people who are going to be celebrating with you and your partner.

The reaction you may get is that one of them won't do anything, that it will probably be the other parent who will cause the trouble. It's amazing how blind people can become to their behavior and how the way that they act can antagonize another person.

Your parents are completely in control of their behavior and how they act towards each other, especially just for one day. That's not a lot to ask at all, and it's perfectly acceptable for you to call them out on it and let them know how you feel.

Weddings can be stressful enough, especially the days leading up to it, and you don't need to be worrying about two grown adults. You need to put your thoughts into the wedding and not them.

So spell it out for them, let them know that if they can't get on for the day, you and your partner would prefer if they didn't come. Also if you have friends or family members who are aware of the situation, see can they help out by keeping them distracted, chat about the fantastic day, have a drink and a dance, and try as best to keep them away from each other.

Hope this works and your parents will see the bigger picture and just be there for you on the day.

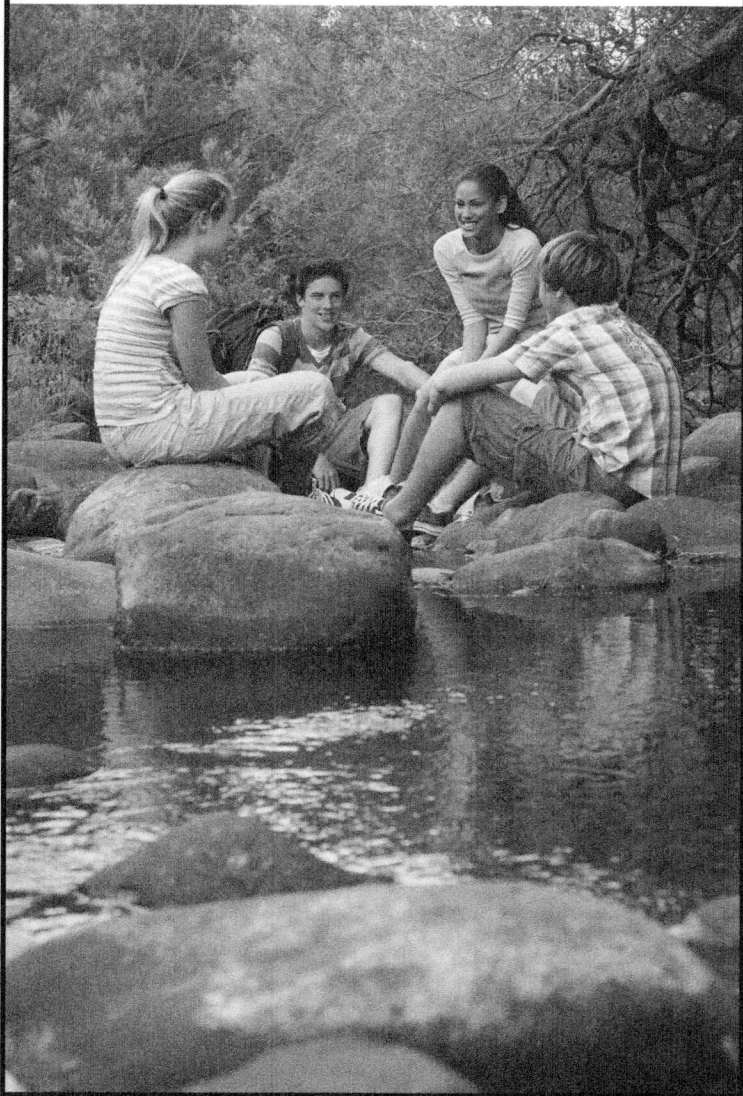

TEENS

Q. I've noticed recently that my fourteen-year-old daughter has been reducing the amount she eats at breakfast every morning. She says parts of the breakfast make her nauseous. I'm worried that it might turn into something bigger. Any advice on how to broach it with her?

A. Over the years working with teenagers, especially girls, they will drop out from sports or exercise around fourteen – sixteen years of age and try to control their weight through their food intake. That's ok if they have a healthy diet, but they will start to cut out the foods and meals that are most important to them.

We are continuously told how important breakfast is; it provides us with energy for the morning, helps regulate our blood sugars, and for children, helps them to concentrate on school subjects early in the day. If we don't have breakfast until later in the morning, let's say around eleven, we've gone nearly twelve or more hours without food, and so, when we do eat, our body feels as if it has been starved and anything we eat will be stored as fat and may not release the energy we need to help us fuel our body for the day ahead.

Unfortunately, we live in a weight-obsessed world, where you can't be too fat or too skinny, and if you are in between, well, you want to make sure you're not going either way. It can be extremely confusing for teenage girls to get this information through social media, magazines, or their peers, and then try to fit in.

It's really important to teach our children and educate ourselves in terms of healthy eating and why it's so important to eat a good diet and, of course, have a little of what you fancy every now and again.

If there are foods that are making your child feel nauseous in the morning, then ask her what she would prefer to eat, and make it clear that she has to have breakfast, but you are happy to have the food she would like to eat in the morning in the house. She's only fourteen, she's going to school, and if she doesn't eat breakfast, she is going to have little energy to concentrate on her classes.

Look at your daughter's exercise, does she do any? Maybe she needs to join a class or gym to get some exercise, but breakfast is really important.

Q. My thirteen-year-old son seems to be completely apathetic about everything. He doesn't get excited about anything—doing things with friends, participating in sports, school. He is doing well in school, so that is not a concern. He's always been a relatively easy-going kid, but in the last six months or so, he seems to have no passion about anything. His older brother tends to get excited and passionate about everything (good & bad) so a more laid-back teen is a nice change of pace. But we would like to see some enthusiasm about something. Is this typical adolescent hormonal behavior, or should we be concerned?

A. It's an age that is really tough for children. They are not young children, but they are not adults, and there are a lot of struggles going on internally in regards to who they are, having control of themselves and their lives, but also needing to abide by rules at home, rules in school. Keep an eye on him, but not so much that he will notice, or that it becomes an obsession for you.

A lot of parents will say "we, or I, want to see them be more enthusiastic." You can want this for your child, but it doesn't mean he will, and it's what you want and not what your child wants. More than likely it is just normal hormonal behaviour, you may just need to let it work its way out of his system. It's possible that he will come out of this phase and be the opposite with a passion for a band or sport or other pastime, and then it will seem as if that's all he will do and talk about!

For now keep an eye on him, but don't get too obsessed about it, and don't put too much pressure on yourself or your son to change or solve the issue. He probably doesn't even see his behaviour as abnormal, he's just getting through a period in his life. If he does seem to be getting worse, more down in himself, then maybe you will need to make a call to your GP for advice.

Q. My son is fifteen and doesn't have a huge group of friends. He doesn't really take part in any sports and has become very moody in the last year. When I try to talk to him about it he says he's fine with the friends he has and has no interest in sports. He loves his depressing music and plays in a band with his friends. I'm just worried that he's missing out on so much as there is so much more to life. How can I get him to see that if he just tries things, he might enjoy them?

A. Sounds familiar! We have to balance what we would like for our children with what they would like for themselves. Not all children are into sports or will be the most popular in class with dozens of friends. Sometimes it's better to have a small amount of close friends than loads of friends as these are usually the people that mean the most and are always there for your child.

Being fourteen–fifteen is a really tough time for a lot of teenagers as you are no longer a child and feel that you should be able to do more adult things. This can be really frustrating for teenagers as they feel they are not being listened to or taken seriously and therefore will be moody and annoyed.

Keep an eye on his behavior. If he is spending time with his friends, writing and playing music, then he is being sociable. It may be a different way than how you would like him to do it, but he is with friends and doing something he is interested in. If our children have a way of expressing themselves, whether it be through music, art, or sport, the most important thing is that they are doing it, it's a release and an opportunity for them to show their individuality.

It's tough being a teenager and even more so now as so much of their lives are lived through social media.

Keep an eye on his diet, make sure he's getting a bit of exercise, and if he is just being a normal teenager and spending time with his friends, then he's probably doing ok.

Be supportive whatever it is he's interested in; your little family is all you need to be concerned with and not what other people think. This phase will pass and hopefully you'll have a son who will be grateful for the way you supported him in all his interests even if they weren't what you would have like him to do. Your relationship will be closer, even if it doesn't feel like it right now.

Q. My daughter is sixteen and about to finish school. She's extremely academic and is quite a bit younger than her classmates finishing. I'm struggling to know what to do about her going to university—not from an academic perspective, but from a maturity one. Do I just let her go or keep her around us for a year?

A. You don't want to hold back your child, even if she is younger than her peers going to college. From my experience of working with children who are academic, they need their minds busy learning. Don't forget your child has probably spent most of her life around older children, so she is used to their behaviours and more than likely, is at a same developmental stage as them because of this.

Sit down with your daughter and have the conversation with her about the future, about college. You may be surprised to learn that she's struggling with the idea of going to college, has worries about being so young in a more adult environment. She may even want to take a year out and stay closer to home. It's best to get her take on everything, too, as it's a big step for her and you want her to feel confident when moving on and know that she can talk to you about this and other issues that may come up in the future. As a parent, your main job was to get your child to the exact point in their lives when they are ready to leave and become adults themselves. You've done this, so now it's time to start seeing her as a young adult and help her with her journey onto the next stage of her life.

As your daughter is academically-minded, she may be so excited to move on to college and challenge herself and her continued learning. She may not be interested in parties, drinking, boys, and is probably more excited about the learning challenges ahead.

She may want to stay close to home for a year, do a one-year course in a local community college and ease herself into the bigger college world. I'm sure you can defer her course for a year if need be. She's not going to be the first sixteen-year-old to go to college. Maybe go to the college she has a place in and see can you have a conversation with someone who looks after new students coming in.

Maybe she could get a job, part-time at least. This will give her a completely different set of life skills and will be great experience when she goes to college and may need to get a part-time job.

It's an exciting time, her whole future ahead of her and lots of options. Life is long, there are many changes in college, careers, this is just the first step.

Q. My fourteen-year-old son has been expelled from school for hitting a teacher. He says the teacher always provokes him and tries to get a reaction, but he shouldn't have hit the teacher. My problem is that none of the schools around us have a space open. We've been told we can get home tuition in the meantime, but I'm really worried he'll get used to not being in school and what might happen then? Already he's staying up much later than usual and laying in in the morning. What can I do to get this all sorted ASAP?

A. As some of you may know, a lot of my day-to-day work is with teenagers. My experience of children who get expelled at this age is that they are in a difficult bubble because they are too young to leave school and get a job, and, in Ireland, by law, they need to be attending school until the age of sixteen. It can be very difficult to find another school willing to take your child in, as places can be limited, and they may not be too keen to have a child that has been expelled from another school for hitting a teacher.

I'm sure you have had a number of conversations with your son's school, so that both sides of the story have been heard, and to try and get their decision reversed. You can appeal this decision, it is worth going down this road, especially if you are going to have difficulty getting your child into another school and if you believe your child deserves another chance.

You will be dealing with an Education Welfare Officer who will be assigned to your son as he is fourteen and has been expelled from school. If home schooling has been offered, this should be taken as it means your son will still be learning and there will be some structure to his day. In my experience the home tuition can be a bit hit-and-miss, but it would be worth doing. Also call on family members who may be able to give him some frequent work, keep him busy, and also offer some guidance. It's amazing how teenagers will listen more to an uncle or aunt or grandparent instead of you! Children I've worked with who do slowly slip into a life of no-structure school seem to move quickly into habits such as smoking, drugs, up all night, and as time goes on, it can be so much harder to pull them back into a normal life.

Children of this age need structure, a reason for being around, and something to be up and out for every day, whether it's school, sports training, hanging out with friends. Your son may be really concerned about the fact that he has been expelled and what it means for the future. He may not be saying anything, but he could be really worried.

So if home schooling hours have been offered, take them regardless of how little there may be. Outside of these hours, see if a family member or friend can give him some work to do, paid or unpaid. If this isn't possible, get him to get some work himself. He will soon start to see how much harder it is to be in the working world where you need to be responsible for yourself all the time.

Keep in touch with the Education Welfare Officer, keep everything moving, and be proactive in getting him back into school. You may need to go to a few schools, discuss your child's needs, and explain that he needs to be in school, and you are there to make sure he works, behaves, and they won't need to worry about a similar incident happening again.

You may have some battles with your son over the next few weeks, but he needs to know that you are the parent, and he needs to take responsibility for his actions. It's not ok to hit a teacher, or anyone for that matter. He is lucky that the guards haven't been involved, and the teacher hasn't taken a case against him.

Q. My fifteen-year-old son was going out with his girlfriend for about nine months. They were really serious, way too serious for my liking, but we've all been there. His girlfriend has recently told him that she wants to break up as she is going away for the summer and thinks it'll be too hard being apart. He is absolutely devastated. We've tried consoling him, but nothing seems to be working. My husband has told him on a few occasions that there's plenty more fish in the sea, but that just seems to make him worse. What can we do to take away his pain?

A. Unfortunately, you can't take the pain away for your son and you shouldn't be trying to either. So much of growing up and learning about life is dealing with the times that test us most, getting through them, and learning coping mechanisms to deal with that situation again in the future. It's a really important time for your son to learn how resilient he really is, live in the pain for a bit, and learn to come out of it feeling ok if not a little bit bruised.

It may take some time for this to happen, and there will be times when you will be really concerned about him, but the best thing you can do is be there for him, tell him it's ok, and that when he's ready to move on he can.

If you broke up with your partner, the last thing you would want to hear is that there are plenty more fish in the sea! It may only have been nine months, but that is a long time in your son's life and especially if it's his first proper relationship. So a bit of patience, love, and support is needed.

Of course it's not ok for your son to be angry with you, or to be acting in a manner in the home that's not acceptable. You are, of course, sympathetic to what's going on, but it's not an excuse to behave in any manner you feel like and make family and home life difficult for everyone.

If, after a few months, you feel your son's mood hasn't improved, you may need to get some advice. If he's closing himself off from friends and family, then you may need to get some counseling for him, an independent ear to hear his feelings and this may help to deal with the loss of the relationship. It's tough being a teenager.

Q. My thirteen-year-old has just started secondary school and has been really looking forward to going to his new school. He has been ready to move since midway through the last school year. It's been a lovely summer, with lots of fun, and a nice holiday in the middle.

I've been checking in with him regularly throughout the summer to see if there is any anxiety as I am very aware of how difficult some students find the transition, but he says he's been feeling absolutely fine about the move as a number of his closest friends were going to the same school also.

It may seem that I'm being picky, but the issue that I have is that he is refusing to take a lunch with him as he says "nobody else does, they all buy their lunch every day." He says bringing in lunch makes him a target for bullies. Obviously, I don't want my child to be a victim of bullying, but, if I'm honest, he is carrying a bit of weight and I don't want it getting worse. He's not big into sports or exercise and I'm worried he'll start to gain even more weight, which will then get him targeted for that, too, by the bullies. Plus there is the financial aspect of giving him money every day, we just can't afford it.

Have you any suggestions on how we can get around this?

A. When I was a kid there was no option but bring your lunch to school, except for the chipper up the road, but it was rare that you could afford a bag of chips!

A lot of schools have started to bring in healthy eating options for the children, and new legislation around the proximity of shops that sell fast food to school is also being brought in.

It's great that your son is transitioning well into secondary school as it can be a really tough time for some children and can take them a couple of years to get to grips with all the changes.

As a parent, a lot of us worry about this time for our children as they are going from being the biggest in one school to being the smallest in another. Thoughts of bullying, not fitting in, and the new but maybe not good experiences they will have, are playing on your mind. You don't know who they will start to hang out with, who will be their new peers. They'll be introduced to people who smoke, maybe drink or do drugs, plus there will be more advanced talk about sex and the opposite sex. For some parents this is a really tough mental time!

From your question this doesn't seem to be too much of an issue for your child as they are settling in well and you don't seem to have noticed a change in them apart from the lunch issue.

Your child is carrying a bit of weight, financially you can't afford to give him money every week, and he is refusing to eat his lunch and you are worried about him getting bullied. So maybe there is a bargaining element here that you can introduce to your child, so having to take lunch to school doesn't seem so bad. Acknowledge what your son is saying to you and that you understand. Explain to him that his health is your responsibility and having a lunch from school every day is not healthy eating. Let him know that financially you wouldn't be able to give him money every day, but maybe there could be a couple of days in the week when he can buy his lunch in school. There could possibly be more days, but in order for any of this to happen, your son needs to take up a sport or start to do some regular exercise outside of school. He may not like this option and tell you to get lost, but you are the parent, his long-term health is your responsibility, and he will have to deal with this new plan. There are so many exercise options out there, it doesn't need to be hours every day, but if he is willing to take this on board, then he will be able to buy his lunch a couple of times a week. This is a trust thing, you need to trust that he is doing the exercise. If you feel he's not keeping up his side of the bargain, then the money gets taken away and he will need to think if it's worth it or not.

Hopefully this will work and be a good balance, but don't put yourself under financial pressure. If you only have money for one day a week then that's all there is. If you are happy with him having two days then maybe he can do a bit for extra work in the house for the extra lunch.

Q. My daughter has literally no interest in school. It has gotten worse and worse every year since she went into secondary school. Arguments are a daily part of the household and I'm finding it harder and harder to manage myself around this. All she says she wants to do is to play music for a living. She says she doesn't see the point in getting a school qualification cause she's never going to go to university and that she is going to make a living at music.

In fairness to her, she works really hard at her music and is literally always tinkering on a guitar or ukulele or the piano. She's very talented but gave up doing music exams as she found it boring and more frustrating than enjoyable.

Obviously, I don't want to be forcing her to do something she doesn't want to do, but I feel she needs to get something else behind her, just in case the music doesn't work out for her. Even if she just finished school, after that I don't really mind what she does.

How do I get her to realise that she needs something behind her…just in case?

A. Firstly, it's great your daughter has a passion for music and really wants it to be her career going forward. Not everyone at her age would see a career path and be determined enough to make sure it happens. For a lot of parents the idea that their child would try to make a feasible living out of music doesn't seem very possible and would be quite negative about this career option.

You have no idea if this is what she will end up doing, neither does your daughter, but you need to stay positive. If your daughter is only fifteen and if you live in Ireland, then there is a legal requirement for her to be in school until sixteen at least. If possible, you need to get your daughter to try and get her secondary school qualification, and then at least if she has this and pursues the music but realises she needs additional qualification, it will be easier for her to apply for a third level course as she will have her final school exams done.

This is a situation where you need to see that your daughter is becoming an adult and needs to be allowed to make some decisions for herself, as long as they fit in with family life and include her finishing school. You may need to do a bit of bartering with her (i.e. finish school), and if she really wants to do music for life, then she could take a year out and give it a real go, but she will need to get a part-time job, too, in order to support herself. After the year, if it's worked out really well, see if there is a course she could do to support her career, most musicians study at some point in their careers, especially if they want to produce their own music and get it into the mainstream market.

Your daughter needs to give you definite plans for her future, how does she see her career developing, and be realistic! Get her to get in touch with music companies, producers, and get an idea of what the music world is really like and how hard she will have to work to get her place in it.

Stay positive. If your daughter puts forward a strong case for doing music as a career, then you need to take it seriously. Make sure she finishes school and then start to put her plan in place for the next year. Ask her to look at all the possible music courses she could enroll in to further or help her career and let her know you are there to support her. Let her know that you will help her, drive her to gigs, help buy equipment, but she needs to get her final school exams, that's the only compromise.

She may only be fifteen, but help her to build her music career now, get her a YouTube channel to post her recordings on. There are other social media outlets, too, that she could use. Get her to do her research on how best to get her music out. Encourage her to enter local talent competitions as all of this will be her CV for the future.

If you give her all these supports and let her know that you will help her, but she is determined not to continue in school, then you need to let her know that you won't be financially supporting her decision. She will need to get a job, support herself, and work on her music. You are not going to let a fifteen-year-old sit around the house, making music, and still be living off you. If at twenty-five or twenty-six she turns around to you, having left school and not got the career she wants, and then realises she needs to do her final exams or look at college courses, then that's her journey and you needed to let her do it. She needs to learn from her own consequences.

It's hard as a parent to see that your child is perhaps not making the best future plans, but you need to stay positive and try and support them as best you can, especially if they are making the effort to support themselves, working hard on what they would like to do. Hard work, determination, and support might just be what's needed for your daughter to pave out her music career, and in the end, whatever happens you will still have a really strong relationship.

TODDLERS

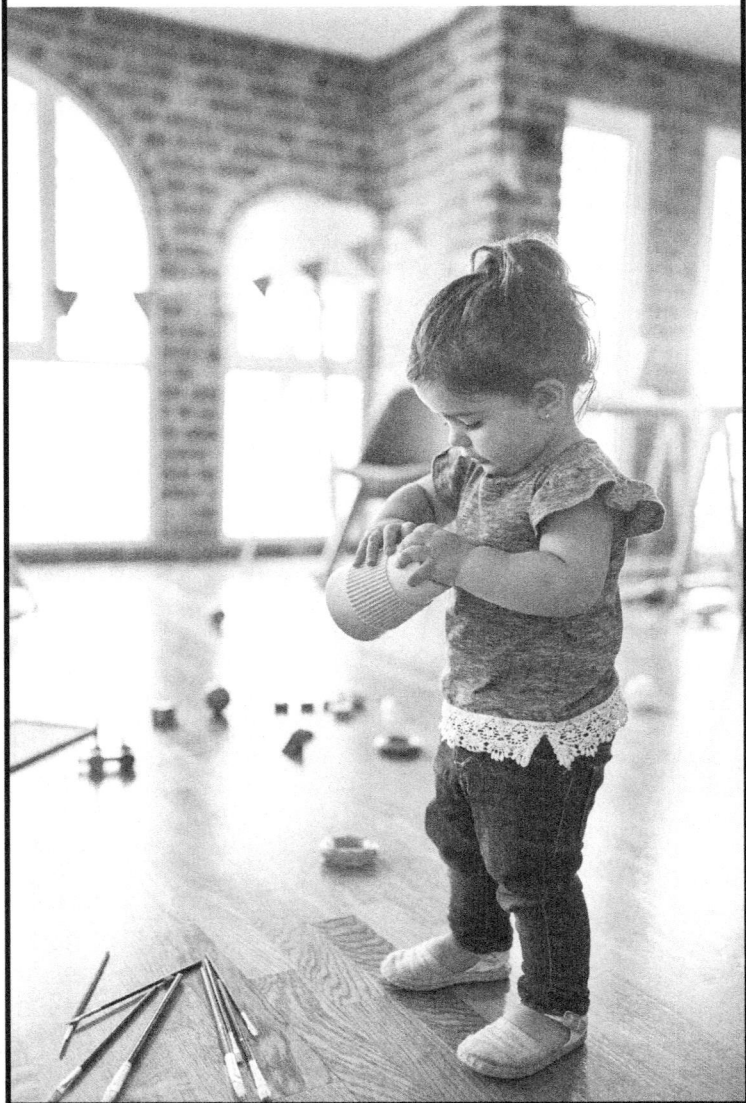

Q. I have two boys, four and two. They're great kids, but recently I noticed my eldest boy is getting more and more boisterous when it comes to playing with his brother. I've spoken to him about being gentle, but he doesn't seem to grasp it. Is there anything I can do to get him to understand?

A. A lot of parents will be able to empathise with your situation. Your eldest son is only four, possibly not in school yet, so still learning how to interact with other children. Your younger son is now two, mobile, and up for loads of fun, and the closest person to him is his big brother. You want to encourage this play as it will lead to lasting bonds between brothers, but it needs to be policed somewhat. You will need to explain to your older son that his younger brother may not be able for the rougher play just yet as they are smaller. Be patient, as he is young, too, and not aware of his own strength when it comes to smaller people. Sit back and see how they play together, if it is getting too rough, then step in and explain what's not right and how they could change the play.

There will, of course, be tears at various stages as they both learn to play properly around each other. If you feel that your older son is being too rough on purpose and fully understands how he needs to play with his brother, then you will need to watch this behavior and perhaps bring in a consequence if he doesn't play properly. He may feel that this is the perfect opportunity to mete out some punishment on his younger brother who is fairly defenseless and unable to verbally let you know what's going on—something to keep in mind.

There will be bumps and knocks, which is normal and part of the rough and tumble of young play. More than likely your younger son will just get up and keep on playing if he gets knocked down, but if you continually correct your older son for every bit of rough play, then your younger son will see this has a way of getting his brother into trouble, and this then changes their relationship. It will bring in distrust, hurt, and could possibly be the start of a number of years of them fighting with each other to get attention or to annoy each other, and don't forget the younger son won't always be small.

Get involved in the play, too, when possible, so you are teaching them as they play and it's more fun. No parent is perfect, we all struggle and don't always get in right, so do what you can, keep them safe, and hopefully it will work out well.

Q. My three-year-old is having a tough time at nursery. She used to love going, but suddenly started getting clingy and crying when we dropped her off. Finally, one night she told me there was a boy at nursery who, in her words, hugged her too tightly and hurt her. It seemed pretty harmless to me, but I asked her teacher about it anyway. My daughter is a little behind in her speech. Because of this she has a hard time communicating, and can be difficult to understand at times, especially if she is upset, so I wanted to make sure I had the facts.

The teacher told me that a boy had grabbed her and started squeezing her, and she pushed him away, and then got upset because she thought she'd get in trouble for pushing. Her teacher said the boy's parents had been told and the situation was under control.

When a week went by and she was still bringing him up every day and crying and not wanting to go to nursery, I spoke to the teacher again and was told that my daughter was terrified of this boy, and rightly so. We both agreed that just taking her out of nursery wasn't the best way to deal with it. She said that they were teaching her tactics to use: to run away as fast as she can whenever she sees the boy, and if he is near her and she feels threatened, to shout as loudly as she can. They think it is good for teaching her resilience.

Now, I'm all for resilience, but I feel that what they are teaching her to do is run away from what scares her. She constantly looks around for him, preparing herself to have to run at a moment's notice. I've seen her (after one of my several meetings with her teacher about this) cowering in the corner just alone by herself because she is too scared to go and play. My idea of resilience is to tell her if a boy is intimidating and laying his hands on her when she doesn't want him, is to punch him in the face, but maybe that's just me? I feel like there has to be a better way to deal with it, I just don't know what it is. The nursery seems to think they have it handled. But she is miserable, so I don't share their opinion. Any advice?

A. That's pretty heavy going. It is a very, very worrying scenario for a number of reasons. Firstly, you don't want your child to be feeling scared about going to crèche. Secondly, you don't want her to learn a life lesson in this manner. You don't want her to feel that running away from matters is going to solve the problem, or that she doesn't feel supported in a situation that isn't right. Also, this isn't fair on the boy, as he's not learning social skills at an age when it's really important to learn what is right and wrong or appropriate or not. This could have a damaging impact on him too. If he is demonstrating possible bullying traits now and he is labelled with this for life, he could struggle for years and not have the proper education or upbringing he deserves. He needs to be taught about the behavior and how what he is doing isn't right and how he could behave towards your daughter.

We all want our children to learn about resilience, to be able to pick themselves back up, deal with a situation, and learn from it for the future. But for me, what's going on with your daughter is not teaching her resilience. Being scared and running away screaming from someone does not help a child understand that the situation is not right and that they can approach an adult who is looking after them and let them know how they are feeling and hope that they will help them. Your daughter is a small child, she needs to feel protected, safe, and it's up to you as a parent and the people you trust to look after her to help her feel this way. It is the job of the people in the crèche to ensure your child's safety and that doesn't matter if it is from another child.

If I were in your shoes, I wouldn't be happy with the situation, especially if my child is that scared of another child and is trying to hide from them and therefore missing out on fun and learning. This must have been heartbreaking for you to hear, and I'm not surprised that you feel you should teach her to punch him if he does it again! Of course, violence is not the answer, and we should never teach our children to use it as a way of getting out of certain situations. More than likely, she will get into more trouble than the boy, and will end up having an even harder time.

I would be concerned about the management of the crèche and how they are teaching the children to behave around each other at play time or other times they are together. If they think this behavior is ok, and it's not something they should be too worried about, then they aren't following proper guidelines. Here in Ireland, the first thing on the list when it comes to working with children is their safety, above anything else. In your case, your daughter is scared, she will, of course, learn some resilience skills out of this, but at the moment she is scared and doesn't feel protected, and that needs to be addressed straight away with the crèche. Maybe they aren't understanding the severity of the situation for your daughter, maybe they don't want to address this issue with the boy's parents.

You need to have another meeting with them, a proper sit down and discuss this situation. Lay out what you, as a parent, feel is appropriate resilience learning and that currently having your daughter run away in fear from another child is not it. Let them know that it's not ok, and put it to them that you need to feel happy about how they are going to handle this. If you feel their answers are not good enough, and that your child may not be protected adequately, then you need to ask yourself if this place is good enough for your child. I know that there is the possibility that this may be the only crèche that is available to you, or maybe there is no availability in other places. You may need to look into this and come up with a possible alternative.

Sit down with your daughter and reassure her that what is happening to her is not right, and that the boy's behavior towards her is not right, and she should always tell the boy no and find someone who can help her. Let the school know that you have said this to your daughter, so if this happens again, she will be calling on them to look out for her and help her.

If this situation doesn't work and the school is not helping, then it may be time to think about lodging a complaint with the local authority. This will take time and maybe you don't want to go that far, but this will continue to be an issue in this school, and even if you take your child out, they will still continue to deal with similar situations in the same way, and it will be another child who suffers. Sometimes you need to stand up and let them know it's not right, not only for your child, but other children and parents who use their facilities.

Put this in the crèche's hands, they need to keep your child safe and decide what they are going to do about the boy who is behaving in an inappropriate way towards your daughter. It's not for you to do, you don't have to have any contact with the other parents as it's the crèche who needs to sort this out.

Hopefully they will take on board what you are saying and will help to sort this situation out for everyone. Hope it works out for you and your daughter.

TWEENS

Q. My ten-year-old just won't keep his room tidy. Even the simple things like tidying away clean clothes or putting stuff in the laundry basket seem impossible tasks. What can I do to get him to realise he has a part to play in keeping the house ticking over and it's pretty simple for him to do?

A. This is such a big problem for most families, and clean bedrooms are nearly impossible. It causes a lot of arguments in families and seems like an endless issue. As a parent, you feel it is your house, and therefore should be kept clean and tidy, but your child will feel that their room is theirs and nothing to do with the rest of the house!

Look at the consequences you have in place at the moment. If they are not keeping their room tidy, maybe they are not enough for your child to notice that you are serious about the issue. You need to let them know that the consequences you will be bringing in will be far worse than the ten minutes they need to spend every day cleaning their room. It doesn't have to be hours of consequences, just enough like fifteen minutes less TV or console time or earlier to bed. Give them a warning, let them know about the consequence, and start small. For the first week get them to make their bed every morning, and this has to continue into the next week when you then get them to hang up their clothes and keep going until it becomes the routine. They will, of course, fall back on some of this, but that's when you bring back in the consequences. Make sure that in the meantime, if they have been sticking to keeping the room tidy, that you praise them and let them know that you are really proud of what they have done. You may need to go through it with them a couple of times so they know how to hang up their clothes, put them in the laundry, or even to make their bed, and then they know what needs to be done and you can leave them to it.

Q. My son has just turned eight and is getting into fights in school. There seems to be no apparent reason for it, and when I ask him he says, "I don't know." The school is concerned, as am I, but he's not telling anyone any reason why. He just told his teacher that one child was looking at him funny and he got angry. What can I do to stop this behavior as I don't want him to get a reputation as a troublemaker? He's really pleasant at home and no real trouble.

A. There is obviously something going on here with your child if he's getting into physical fights and he's struggling to control his anger and his behaviour when it comes to recognising socially acceptable behaviour. He is only a child and this may need some investigating. He may be feeling stressed, there could be something going on in the class, or perhaps home life is a bit chaotic for some reason and he's unable to regulate or express how he is feeling and the frustration is turning into rage.

Take some time to see what is going on in his day-to-day life, get in touch with the school and ask them how he is behaving most of the week. It's important to look at the home life, too, and see are there things going on that are making him feel stressed. Sometimes we are so busy trying to get from one day to the next that we don't see that are children are struggling to keep up. They can become overwhelmed and under pressure if they are being shouted at all the time because they are not doing things fast enough. Is there downtime for your child after school or in the evenings instead of being rushed from school to after school activities? If this is happening in your home, you will be feeling under pressure and tired, so he, too, may be feeling this way.

If you haven't been experiencing this anger in the home, you will need to let the school know and ask them to help you to better understand what it happening in the school as you have not witnessed the behaviour yourself. Perhaps get their advice and come up with a plan together to find something to work for him.

If he has access to the internet or a device, look at what he is playing.

Is this something that might be affecting his behaviour?

If he is struggling to verbalise how he is feeling, perhaps get him a notebook to write down what's going on inside or draw out how he is feeling. It may only be a line or two, or something small, but it could help. Get him to write about his day and then you can write down about your day. This really helps if the day is busy and you're not getting proper time to catch up. If you get to read how his day was and he reads about yours, when you do get a moment together, you can talk about it. It may help your son to process what happened in the day, good or bad, and they will see that the one bad incident in the day is a very small part of the day.

If the behaviour continues, and you can't understand what is causing the anger, then you may need to bring in consequences. He needs to be aware that being violent towards another child is not acceptable and that he will have to deal with consequences such as no devices, if he doesn't start to control his behaviour. The consequences need to be enough that it will stop your child and make them think about what they could be losing out on if they decide to keep behaving the same way.

If all of the above hasn't helped, you may need to look at getting some professional help, there could be more going on.

So, look at the supports you have, talk to the school, and try the notebook.

Q. My nine-year-old daughter has started to put on quite a bit of weight. I struggle myself, too, but I'm really worried about her as I don't want her to have to deal with what I have through my life. I find it so hard to say no to her when she looks for treats as I don't want her upset. What can I do to get her eating healthily?

A. It's good that you've noticed that your child has put on a bit of weight and that you would like to do something about it, so that she doesn't have weight issues in the future. The fact that you have had your own struggles with weight could be a positive for everyone, and maybe you could all do something as a family to improve your diets.

Firstly, it would be a good idea to rid the house of any unnecessary treats such as chocolate, biscuits, crisps, fizzy drinks. This is not easy, especially if daily treats are normal and you enjoy the odd biscuit with your cuppa. A lot of people give themselves treats as a form of reward for getting to the end of the day or if their child has done something good in school, and it's not a good way to reward as ultimately it's doing more harm than good.

It's so much easier for everyone if you decide to make these changes together as a family and everyone is on board. It would be unfair for one child to continue to get daily treats and another doesn't, or for your partner to eat biscuits in the evening while you are trying to stay away from them.

Banning treats from the house altogether is not a good idea either, we all need a little of what we fancy, so making the weekends the time for a bar of chocolate or a favourite dessert makes it really special and so much more enjoyable. Over time this will become normal and it will be easier to say no during the week to the treats. Special occasions like birthdays, Christmas, are also a time to enjoy, but just not to over indulge as you could be starting from step one again.

You are in control of what your child eats, so you have a lot more control than you think, and although she will not be happy initially if you keep the new changes in place, she will eventually get on board.

When it comes to meals, and if you are cooking, have a look at what you are eating. If you are pushed for time, can you prepare the night before or do a bit of cooking together at the weekend? Home-cooked meals can be just as tasty and satisfying as take away.

Look at the exercise your daughter does every day. Most nine-year-old children, unless they have a medical condition, should not be overweight as they should be doing enough running around to burn off all the calories they consume.

If she is sitting for long periods and eating, you will need to stop this. Look at activities she may be interested in doing outside of school, such as swimming, dance, gymnastics, and get her involved. Also look at going walking or jogging together, it's time spent together and you will both really enjoy it.

It's really important to teach your child what a healthy lifestyle is, and most children learn through what they see their parents doing. This will take a bit of work and planning, but small changes over the next few weeks will make big changes for your family in the future.

Q. My ten-year-old son cannot make up his mind what he wants for his birthday. We are on a budget financially, but can afford a party or a present for him. He keeps going back and forth with wanting a big, not-too-cheap party with his friends, and we have explained that that will mean his present is smaller. He then flops to wanting a bigger present and smaller party, and then back and forth and back and forth. We need to make a decision as his birthday is in three weeks, and I need to organise things. I want him to understand the value of money, but I also need to get shit organised! What can I do to get him moving?

A. Tricky one! This is when you need to set a deadline with your son and it's non-negotiable, he needs to decide big party/small present or the other way around. That's the cut-off point, and if he doesn't decide, then the decision will be made by you, the parents. Sit him down, explain to him that you need time to be able to organize a party and let his friends know, so that they will be free on the day, especially as children are so busy these days. This may give him enough of a push to make his mind up either way and then, hopefully, it will be plain sailing to a very happy and enjoyable birthday.

Q. My nine-year-old daughter just seems to want to fight with everyone around her. She's been getting into trouble in school for getting into arguments and she constantly seems ready for a fight at home. If we ask her to do anything she goes from nought to sixty in the blink of an eye. We're all tired, including her, of the arguments, but she just can't seem to control her temper. Her dad is very similar, and they clash a lot, which leaves a lot of tension in our home. Have you any suggestions as to how we can get her to change her behaviour?

A. This is tough and tiring for everybody in the house. It is mentally and physically tiring having arguments in the house, especially if they are happening regularly. You are always dealing with stressful situations outside of the home, too, as your daughter is getting into trouble in school, and you have to deal with teachers too. You are then in a situation where you feel you have to correct your child and she is waiting for it to happen as she knows she did something wrong. All of this leads to tension. Everyone will have their backs up and ready for the fight that is inevitably going to happen.

Has this behavior been going on for a long time? Has your daughter always been argumentative, even from a young age? How is your family situation at the moment? If you could imagine yourself looking into your family as someone from the outside, would you say the atmosphere is relaxed and happy? This isn't a criticism, it's just a chance to look back and see if the tension has always been there. You mentioned your husband has a similar personality to your daughter, has this caused issues in the house over the years?

Your daughter may just have gotten used to living in an environment where there has been tension, and this is her default and the way she behaves when things don't go right because she doesn't know how to act any other way.

If this isn't the case, maybe there's more going on in your daughter's life that you are not aware of. It could be a mental health issue, perhaps she has trouble recognizing emotions or being emotional towards other people. Does she show any empathy towards people or even pets, if you have one? If you think that maybe there is something else going on that you can't put your finger on, it may be worth taking her for an assessment, it can't do any harm. If she had a pain or was sick you would take her to the doctor and get a diagnosis. This is no different, and if nothing comes back, then you may need to look at other supports for your daughter. But if something does come back, you will be able to understand your daughter's feelings and emotions better, and it will be a great starting point, it not a tough one at first, to help deal with your daughter in a calmer way.

If you really don't think this is the issue, then you may need to look at the boundaries you put in place when your child is misbehaving. Sometimes when we have children who are very willful and we are tired at the end of the day, or we just can't deal with them, we can tend to let them get away with behavior that probably isn't acceptable. In not correcting children who behave in this way, we are allowing them to get away with it and they will push more, and their behavior can become worse.

If you decide to bring in consequences for your daughter, this will take time. It needs to be consistent, and also it has to be in line with the misbehavior. By this I mean if your child has shouted at you, there is no point in banishing her to her room for the rest of the day with no tv, the consequence has to be on the same level as the misbehavior.

When we see anger in another person it is usually masking another emotion such as fear, upset, or anxiety. She may be trying to tell you something through her behavior. Although it may not be the right way to do, she may just not be able to express herself any other way. Take some time to look at her day-to-day life. Could there be something going on in school? Is she getting enough nutrition and exercise in the day? Has she friends she can rely on?

You may need to look at some professional help, it may only be a few sessions, but it might give you both a break. It will give your daughter an opportunity to speak to someone impartial, and will give you time to come up with a plan of action for the future.

What are your daughter's interests? Is there a hobby that you can get her involved with, something maybe the two of you could do together? There will be time needed to sort this situation out, but as a parent, our child's mental development and wellbeing are really important, and that is your number one job. Housework, tv, can wait—this is something that is really important for your daughter.

Even if you do put time aside for her and she doesn't engage, don't get discouraged. You are using this as an opportunity for her to talk if she wants, but it's also good for her to have time with you or both parents.

Look at the boundaries and consequences, keep them consistent, and make sure both parents are doing the same thing. Let your daughter know how much you love her and how you think she is great, even if she doesn't want to hear it. While your child is going through this tough time, it's important to protect her and doesn't get labelled as a "bad child." We all have tough times and make mistakes, but we need compassion and understanding at these times too.

Acknowledgements

Yet again, thank you so much to Julie for transcribing the book, reviewing it, and basically making it what it is. Thanks also to my girls, Amie-Mai & April, for being so caring, understanding and keeping y feet grounded in what's really important. Maria Fowler deserves a statue to be built because of what she has had to put up with while going through this process with me. To all my family and friends, I love you all!

And to everyone who bought the first book and preordered this one, it means more to me than you will ever know!

Parenting in My Pocket Q & A Volume 1

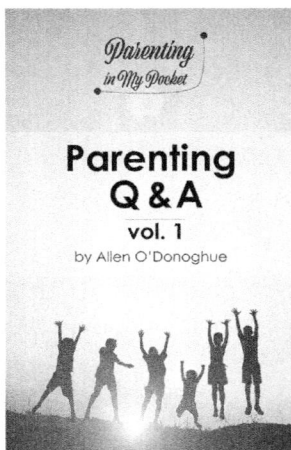

Asking for help when it comes to parenting can be difficult, but we all need help from time to time. Taken from his live Q & A shows, highly regarded family coach and speaker, Allen O'Donoghue, answers your most pressing parenting questions in the first book of the Parenting in My Pocket series. Allen approaches each question with insight, empathy, practicality, no judgement, and a dash of humour. Topics in volume 1 include:

• Activities • Anxiety • Being a Parent • COVID-19 • Dealing with Conflict • Exams & Education • Grief & Loss • Managing Behaviour • Safety (On and offline) • Separation & Divorce • Toddlers • Tweens and Teens

Parenting in my Pocket Q & A Volume 1 is available online through Amazon (US & UK), Barnes & Noble, and Waterstone's Booksellers. Signed copies can be ordered through the Help Me to Parent website.

Reviews for Parenting in My Pocket Q & A Volume 1

As a mother of three (aged eighteen, fifteen and ten) I thought I had navigated the roller coaster that is parenting fairly well over the years without the need for outside help, but then Covid hit and my husband went overseas for six months. I was so pleased to discover not only Allen's podcasts, FB lives, but also this book. Allen has such a wealth of experience and is never patronising in the advice that he offers (my personal pet hate). This book has given me the confidence to set boundaries again and follow up with the consequences so my fifteen-year-old now respects me far more and no longer tries to rule the house with his older brother at Uni and his dad away. The other sections are equally illuminating and give you some comfort that you are not the only one going through these trials. It feels like I have someone on my side! ~*Louise B.*

●————●

I've long been a fan of Allen's articles, podcasts, and online parenting courses. I cannot tell you how much I've learned over the last many years from following Allen and Help Me to Parent on social media, email distributions, and taking his courses. This book does not disappoint. Allen has wonderful, practical, advice for so many parenting challenges. His tips are easily implemented and can be slowly introduced to your day to day routine. It all feels doable, nothing drastic but even the smallest changes make such a significant impact on day-to-day life. His work has had such an impact on my kids' lives, I cannot recommend this book enough, along with Help Me to Parent and Allen's parenting coaching. It's so lovely to have his advice on paper where you can reference it anytime you need it! Buy this book!! ~*L.*

●————●

Allen has saved my parenting sanity on countless occasions. I am so pleased that he has made his practical and genuinely helpful advice available in a format that I can refer back to as needed. His weekly Q&A podcast is available on multiple platforms and is the perfect supplement to the topics covered. In addition to addressing typical parenting concerns like toddlers, tweens & teens, Allen has included questions on anxiety, electronics and issues related to school—and even COVID-19. This is titled as Volume 1 which gives me hope for many more coming our way in the future! ~*Lisa M*

Allen O'Donoghue

Allen is a professional coach, trainer and facilitator with over twenty years of experience in youth and family development. With qualifications in Transactional Analysis Psychotherapy, Social Science and Logosynthesis®, Allen's specialist knowledge and understanding of family dynamics has supported hundreds of young people and adults in setting and achieving their personal goals.

This experience has brought Allen to become a highly regarded speaker on family coaching, appearing regularly on radio and presenting at international events.

Allen also runs the highly successful Business & Life Coaching company CA Coaching www.cacoaching.ie

About Help Me To Parent

Help Me To Parent opened its doors to parents in 2007 to great success. Through constant research and development, our programmes have consistently stayed ahead of the curve in providing practical, dynamic, and ultimately easy-to-use content, that parents can put in place as soon as they get home.

With over one hundred years combined experience in providing support to individuals and families, the Help Me To Parent team have a wealth of experience to meet any needs that parents, children, or soon-to-be parents have.

Our extensive portfolio of programmes and courses are tried and tested and have received the seal of approval from the hundreds of families we have worked with over the years.

You can find us at http://helpme2parent.ie/

Printed in Great Britain
by Amazon